A BOOK

DESTINED to WIN

Volume 4

Pierced for a Purpose

Tammy Vaughan

Printed in the United States of America
ISBN: 979-8-9851725-7-7
Copyright © 2021 Tammy Vaughn

Library of Congress Cataloging-in-Publication Data

Scripture quotations are taken from the Holy Bible, New Living Translation (NIV), copyright © 1996, 2004, 2007, 2013, 2015 by Tyndale House Foundation.
All rights reserved.

Compilation Book Coaching: SynergyEd Consulting/ synergyedconsulting.com
Graphics & Marketing: Greenlight Creations Graphics Designs
Book Cover: MyAsia Reed
www.glightcreations.com/ glightcreations@gmail.com

sheropublishing.com
getpublished@sheropublishing.com

A BOOK COMPILATION

DESTINED to WIN
Volume 4

Pierced for a Purpose

Table of Contents

~Co-Author Chapters~

Dedication

This book is dedicated to those who have been pierced from the trials of life to the point where they thought they would never be able to put themselves back together, but they overcame!

Some of us have been pierced to the point where we wanted to quit. I want to suggest that there's nothing wrong with feeling like quitting. All of us feel like quitting, at some point in life, but don't give up! You fought too hard, prayed too long, fasted too much, suffered too long, endured too much, and come too far. The worse is behind you and the best is in front of you.

Remember this…Jesus healed two men possessed with demons. He raised a little girl from the dead. He healed the woman with the issue of blood. He opened blinded eyes. He healed a mute man. No matter what you have faced, my prayer is that these stories show you that Jesus can restore all and make all things anew.

~Pierced for a Purpose

Acknowledgments

I would like to thank all the midwives, in my life, who assisted me in pushing this baby forth. To my family, thank you for always believing in me. I couldn't do any of this without your love and support.

To the SHERO Publishing staff; Erica Perry Green, Camilla Moore, and our amazing book coach, Kimberly Perry Sanderlin, the editors, graphics, and marketing team, thank you for keeping us on the right track.

Lastly, I would like to thank each Co-Author for your dedication to my vision. Thank you for your strength and courage to share your story and journey to bless others. I salute you and pray that, in all you do, you remember that you are **Destined to Win**!

In Honor of:

I want to take a moment to thank two very special people who have gone on to be with the Lord.

To the late (great) Deacon Samuel Hightower; Sir, you always told me to tell my story because somebody needs to hear it. Well Sir, I got sixteen other people to tell theirs. *Rest well Sir.*

To my spiritual mother, the late (great) Pastor Ruth E. Wilson. Thank you for always believing in me, even when I didn't believe in myself. I miss you dearly.

Introduction

The purpose of this book is to share the stories and journeys of women and men who have gone through the fire but remained "unburned" because of God's love, grace, and mercy. Throughout these stories of adversity and overcoming, each author will share how they were **Pierced for a Purpose** in the hopes that they can help to encourage or inspire someone else, as they press through.

My Prayer for
Your Reading Journey

Father God,

I come to You as humbly as I know how, thanking You for the person who is preparing to read this book. I pray, that You will allow them to have an open and receptive heart, and that every word they read, will begin the journey of healing for them.

I pray that each chapter will assist them in every way possible; spiritually, personally, and mentally. Mend those *Pierced for a Purpose.* I pray that every time they pick up this book to read, they feel your presence. Father, most of all, I pray that this book will help them become all that You've created them to be.

I thank You, in advance, for Your healing power that is going to manifest through every page in this book and I ask You for these and all other blessings, in Jesus' name.

Amen

~ The Visionary

Author Chapters

Author Annette Edwards-Lewis

Author Annette Edwards Lewis

Annette Edwards Lewis was born to her parents, Emma L. Goodman and Leroy Hodges Sr., in Newark, New Jersey. She grew up with eight brothers, five sisters, and one precious niece.

Annette resides in Boston, Massachusetts. She is a wife, mother of two sons, and grandmother of one precious grandson. Annette is a child of God and loves to encourage and help people. She has obtained her Associate, Bachelor of Arts, and Masters in Early Childhood Education. She has experienced a full and rewarding career in the field of Early Childhood Education. In her spare time, Annette loves to read, color, do puzzles, and sudoku.

Connect with author Annette Edwards Lewis:
Email: margarq911@gmail.com

Forgiveness to Freedom
(One of Daddy's Little Girls)
"Your Grace and Mercy brought Me Through"

Forgiveness is something I struggled with ever since I was a little girl. As a child, I learned to get over people hurting me real fast. When you are young it may matter for a moment, but for me, I moved on. As I got older, I noticed that it became harder to forgive people for the ways they hurt me. I just couldn't understand how people could constantly hurt you and not think anything of it, even if you confronted them about it.

I suppressed a lot of my feelings, from childhood to adulthood. I did things to make people laugh, but on the inside, I was literally dying. I have forgiven people but have never forgotten. I just refuse to accept their madness any longer. Growing up I struggled with forgiveness toward my biological dad. Let's just say, I always thought he didn't care for me much, and his actions were loud.

As much as I wanted to have a loving and caring relationship with my dad, it never took place. I basically went along to get along. My dad was tough, but I wasn't sure if that was his way of showing love. My dad always seemed to treat me differently than my sister. I never understood why. I used to always say to my sister, "I wish I had a relationship with dad like you did."

Yes, as a little girl, it was confusing. I would always find myself asking the question, "Why?" I thought something was wrong with me. I didn't feel good enough. I tried my best, as a kid, to do the right things, to get good grades, but it didn't really help. Sometimes, when my dad would come around, he would say things like, "You are special" or "You are different", but in a negative tone. I took that with me into my adulthood. I thank God for my mom who tried her best to help me *understand* my dad. However, most of the time, he didn't seem very nice to me.

When I was 14 years old, my dad and I had an ugly argument that led us to stop speaking to each other for seven years. I dealt with it, but I just could not understand how a father could just live his life and not speak to his daughter over a disagreement. That was so mindboggling to me and those were some crucial years in my life when I wished my dad was around. I truly thank God for my stepdad who took us as his daughters and was very present in our lives. I know he had his hands full with us and my niece, but at least he tried.

By the time I was 21 years old, my older sister had invited me over to visit her place. I took a chance because it was my dad's house. She lived upstairs from my dad. As I was leaving her house my dad was sitting on his couch with the door open. By that time, he had become a minister. So instead of him saying, "Hi", he quoted a scripture to me- *Honour thy father and thy mother: that thy days may be long upon the land which the Lord thy God giveth thee. Exodus 20: 12 (KJV).*

Well, thank God I grew up in Sunday School; I was able to quote a scripture back to him- *And ye, fathers, provoke not your children to wrath: but bring them up in the nurture and admonition of the Lord.* (Ephesians 6: 4 KJV). I know he didn't like it, but that was all I had.

We slowly started to talk a little, but I kept my guard up and was careful not to get too comfortable with him. He never apologized and I thought that was odd, now that he was a minister. I was very respectful despite how he treated me.

To set the record straight, my dad did do things for me, he didn't totally abandon me, but sometimes in my life it sure felt like it. Just being honest. Later in my life, I started working in a bank as a teller. One of my coworkers invited me to church on a Friday night and I said, "Yes". She was so nice, she picked me up to make sure I got there. This was the week before Christmas in 1987, and I don't exactly know what happened to me when I went up for prayer, but I must honestly say, I was not the same person the next day, after giving my life to Christ! That Sunday, I attended Morning Star Church of God in Christ, in Newark New Jersey. It was the church I used to attend when I was a little girl. It was such a blessing to see that the same people that I knew from my childhood were still in the church, and there were new members. My son and I joined the church that Sunday!

I stayed at Morning Star Church of God in Christ for some years, and then my dad established a church, Strangers Home Church of God in Christ, in Irvington New Jersey. I left Morning Star to go help my dad in his church; I remained at my dad's church until I remarried and moved to Boston, Massachusetts. I was the first wedding my dad performed in his church and that was a blessing. I worked in the church and in a daycare that he had in the lower part of the church during the week. So, I was basically at church most of the time. I didn't always agree with my dad, but I let him handle his church affairs and helped the best I could. I was a Sunday School teacher, and I loved every moment of it.

As I lived my new life in Boston, I would often return to New Jersey to see my family and friends. I would visit my dad's church from time to time. I also kept in touch with my dad through my sister. In 2003, I lost my mom and that was very devastating, but God had prepared me for it. I had lost three brothers, one sister, both grandparents on each side, aunts, and uncles, cousins, two stepdads, my niece, and great-nephew that were very dear to me. Through those losses God kept me.

Well into my adulthood, and two years after my mom passed, I had this burning desire to talk to my dad. He was the only parent I had left, and I really needed to say what I felt needed to be said and to free myself. I really prayed about going to talk to my dad, and I wanted it to be just me and him. So, as I was driving to New Jersey, I was rehearsing what I was going to say and how I was going to say it. I didn't want to say the wrong thing and we get into an argument again, so I wanted to choose my words wisely. After all, my dad was a pastor and I wanted to respect him and not be a threat to him in any way.

When I arrived, my dad was alone. I was so thankful to God that it was just me and him in the house. That rarely happened to me since I have a lot of siblings. I believe God made this time just for me. I was a little nervous, but I came to speak my truth. I came in, we sat down, and I told my dad I really wanted to talk to him about some things that have bothered me all my life. I began talking and the more I talked the less nervous I became. I asked some questions that I needed some clarity on.

The good part about this conversation was that this was the first time that my dad was quiet and listened to every word I had to say. He let me continue speaking, and he answered my questions accordingly. I thought before I spoke because a lot of what I was saying was coming from a place of hurt. I had needed my dad to be there for me. But on this day, all I wanted was for him to just *listen*.

I said one last thing to my dad, and suddenly it got very quiet in the room, and when I looked at my dad, a tear ran down his cheek. Now, in my mind, I was thinking, "Girl, you done messed up now! He is going to ask you to leave and never come back to his house again!" Plus, I had never seen my dad cry, so I just knew I had struck a nerve, and it was going to turn for the worse. For a moment there was just silence.

When my dad finally spoke, he said, "Out of all of my children, you were the only child I could not reach. I asked God, 'how do I reach my child?' The Lord said, 'She does not want your money; she wants your love.'" Again, there was just silence; but his words *felt* so good. Then he said, "You were a beautiful baby when you were born. You never gave me any trouble and you didn't ask for anything."

In 2011, my dad had surgery and I decided to take a week off and go to New Jersey and give my family a little break and help take care of him. Now, I really had to pray about this because I have never stayed over in my dad's house that he had with the church. It was going to be an experience for me. But I was committed; I was going there to spend time with my dad and take care of him.

When I say prayer works, trust me it really does. Now I was like a little girl who was having the time of her life with her dad; just the two of us. It felt good, and this would be the first time ever that it would just be me and my dad for a whole week together. He prayed over me as soon as I got there. This was going to be an interesting week for me. My dad is a storyteller, and he had a lot of stories to tell that I had never heard before. We laughed, cried, and laughed some more. I enjoyed making breakfast, lunch, and dinner for my dad every day.

He would share stories of him and his family growing up in Mississippi. My dad was a go-getter, and he wasn't afraid to take a risk on things. He was a business owner too and did well with it for many years. I enjoyed our morning tea or coffee time as he held my hand while he told me a different story each day. I prayed every day that we would have a good day together and God blessed us.

As I spent those days with my dad, God began to soften my heart. I do not remember the day, but one day I was sitting on the couch and my dad was just talking away and telling me about my grandfather, grandmother, my great-grandfather, and my aunts and uncles. Then he would break out in a song, and I would just be in awe with his singing. Back in the day, my dad had a band, and he played the guitar.

I began to look at my dad, and as I was looking at him, I saw a soul. I can't really explain it to you, but it was a warm feeling that came over me, and every negative thing that I thought of my dad was washed away. That is when I knew I had forgiven my dad for every hurt and pain he had caused me in my life. I held back the tears and went to the bathroom and cried like a baby. It was such a relief to know that I was no longer was bound by anger towards my dad!

God had orchestrated that time just for me. Later that night when my dad went to bed, I cried out to the Lord and said, "Thank You". I know I didn't have to go around feeling less than or not enough, because I was totally delivered. In so many words, my dad apologized to me the best way he knew how, and I accepted it. I have a sister who would say, "Daddy did the best he could with what he had." And I guess he did.

Forgiveness can be done, but for me, it took a long time. I was 50 when this change came into my life. I know they say- *better late than never.* For me, it was a long time to hurt.

It has been a long journey, but with God, I was able to get through it. There have been others that have hurt me as well, but I was able to forgive them and move on from it. No love lost on my part, it only made me stronger. It took a while too, but I am totally delivered from their madness as well. I know this was a lesson learned, but it took me forever to get it all figured out.

My advice to anyone who is trying or wants to forgive someone, I would suggest praying about it and letting God do the work in you. Most of the time, people are not even aware that they have violated you in any capacity. For some people, it's just their nature to hurt you and not even care because they are selfish. Then there are some people who just really don't care about hurting your feelings because it doesn't affect them. So why bother. Avoid toxic people at all costs. I know that could be hard if it's a family member, but they are not exempt when it comes to your sanity.

I am telling some of my story because I want someone to know there is always hope. A daughter longs for a connection with her dad. He is the first man in her life. He is supposed to nurture, love, support, and be there for her. I know that may not always be the case, but it would be such a blessing if it was. It would sure help a girl or woman to stop searching for love in all the wrong places. My story also lets you know that even though I forgave my dad, there are dads out there that can ask for forgiveness as well. Forgiveness can go both ways and God can bless and heal that relationship.

I know if he did it for me, God can do it for you as well. You must have a willing mind to let go of that which has you bound. Unlike me, don't let anyone hold you hostage and keep you in bondage emotionally. They are living their best life and you are holding onto anger because of how they treated you. LET IT GO! Enough is enough. Get people out of your head and live your best life too. You can go from *Forgiveness to Freedom* like I did.

Notes On Overcoming:

_____

_____

_____

_____

_____

_____

_____

_____

_____

Author Dana Reeves

Author Dana Reeves

Dana Reeves was born to Pearl and Carl Reeves in Durham, North Carolina. She professed her faith in Jesus and was baptized at a very early age. Dana's parents were dedicated to not losing their children to demonic influences. But like most families, they were always haunted by the legacy of poverty, substance abuse, and crime that plague the neighborhoods of Durham. Dana watched friends being physically attacked, raped, locked away, and eventually murdered before she realized that there was nothing thrilling or entertaining about the realities of street life. Although she often witnessed a hostile external environment, she knew that God was real. Her parent's home was the center of refuge for children and would be the beginning of her dedication to helping families and children

At the age of fifteen, her parents made the brave decision to place Dana in Durham's Camelot Academy. It was there that she learned to focus on academics and eventually graduated from Camelot Academy as Class Valedictorian.

In 1994, Dana attended college at Western Carolina University, where she received a Bachelor of Science in Child Development and Family Relations. She has spent twenty-five years as a Child Development Professional in Christian and non-profit organizations. Dana has served in various roles as a Youth Advocate, Youth Pastor, Children's Ministry Director, Master Teacher, Education Coordinator, and Program Coordinator. In 2002, she became a single mother to Leah Reeves and began her calling to motherhood. Not until she became a mother, did she realize the importance of a biblical worldview and the importance of the mission of Christian Education. Dana is currently employed by Yates Baptist Childcare Center as a Preschool teacher. Dana has earned a master's degree in Christian Ministry from Bethel Bible College and Seminary. She is currently working on a Doctorate in Christian Education.

In 2011, Dana answered the call of Ministry on her life at Victorious Life Fellowship Church under the teaching of Bishop Darion White. Dana is currently a licensed Minister at Celebrations Ministries Lutheran serving as Youth Pastor under the leadership of Apostle Bishop Dr. Rhonda Hatton and Bishop Ian Hatton. Dana was appointed to serve as Marketing Administrator and Director of Children and Young Adults for Royal PriestHood Fellowship of Churches. Dana currently serves as a Professor at Royal Theological Seminary, Durham, North Carolina.

To connect with Dana Reeves:
Email: Danareeves431@gmail.com

From the Trap House to God's House

"So, what's the drug game like?"

He was referring to the drug scene in the small, secluded college town of Cullowhee, North Carolina. A place that I would be leaving slightly disappointed that God had not given me all that I was entitled to and deserved. I wanted out of that place. It had served its purpose. I knew that asking this question, was his way of letting me be a part of his world, even if it was illegal. To everyone else, I had everything. Yet, in reality, my life was coming apart at the seams! I had spent my college years in a complete tail-spin, complete with mental exhaustion, weed smoking, and religious fervor. I was making plans to leave it all behind and return home to Durham, North Carolina. I knew that he was awaiting my return. He had an amazing ability to make me feel safe and exposed, all at the same time. We were now two misfits on a dangerous collision course of murder and deception.

I replied firmly, "I'm in college and working, how am I supposed to know that?

I gave a nervous laugh in order to deescalate the moment. My heart was pounding in my chest. I knew that my answer was a loyalty test. We had known each other since middle school, in fact, he was my first car date. My ghetto Prince Charming arrived in a lowered Ford Crown Victoria with big rims, met my father, even opened the door for me. Dutch Had always been a "bad boy" but that was the case for most of the boys I grew up with. I wanted to pass his test and prove myself to him. I patiently listened to his husky breathing on the other end of the phone line. His voice sounded more intense and powerful than I remembered.

"So, when are you coming home?" he whispered.

Although his words were soft there was nothing gentle about his question. I felt the presence of danger; something had changed. We had unspoken rules between us; we never discussed plans for our future. We simply had an understanding. We chose to be together with no titles or commitment. We were completely free to carve out our own path. I knew that he was not the "one", but a temporary replacement. I had endured multiple relationships with fake "nice guys". I had grown tired of being blindsided by gut-wrenching breakups. I wasn't fully devoted to our *situationship*. I wasn't in love with him. I just loved the newfound attention he gave me. I was tired of feelings of rejection and couldn't comprehend his devious motives for this new interest. Perhaps he sensed my internal demons: my feelings of being inadequate and undeserving. I knew that his girlfriend had recently died from mysterious reasons. He chose not to talk about it, I chose not to question him. Our puppy love was now a full-grown *situationship*. I felt more secure with him than anyone else in the entire world. I decided to mock his new attempt at showing affection towards me.

"Why, do you miss me?" He responded with a nervous laugh.

Honestly, it unnerved me, but I ignored it like so many other warning signs. I was coming home to my childhood friend. He was no longer "a bad boy", in every sense of the word he was now a "bad man".

Be alert and of sober mind. Your enemy the devil prowls around like a roaring lion looking for someone to devour. - 1 Peter 5: 8, New International Version

The more time I spent with him the more I learned that he was no longer the street-corner dope boy, but a cold-blooded, calculated kingpin. I turned a blind eye to how he lived his life. He had mastered smuggling large shipments of drugs and proudly told me more than I should know. It was normal to see a bathtub full of marijuana, pornography playing on the big screen TV, and guns. Young boys would show up with empty book bags and disappear to the backroom, and then quickly leave with a full book bag. In the main room, there was loud music, a thick fog of weed smoke, and the smell of stale malt liquor. It was obvious that he was running a trap house. A trap house "is a place where people go to buy drugs. It is a place rented by the main person or a group of people who are involved in the business of illegal drug deals." The neighbors were oblivious to his operations and illegal activities. In fact, Dutch preferred secrets and deception.

You belong to your father, the devil, and you want to carry out your father's desires. He was a murderer from the beginning, not holding to the truth, for there is no truth in him. When he lies, he speaks his native language, for he is a liar and the father of lies. - John 8:44, New International Version

Mayhem was a normal occurrence for Dutch and his loyal crew. He wanted to live fast and die young. I would listen for hours as they traded battle stories. Who got arrested? Who got shot or stabbed. Everyone seemed so impressed that Dutch had been shot multiple times; I found it terrifying. My uncles died violent deaths, and even my grandma hustled. Seeing loved ones locked away, physically attacked, raped, and murdered was generationally woven into both our narratives. I knew all too well that this life had an expiration date. He reveled in the chaos I felt trapped in. I no longer wanted to live in two contradicting realities. I was afraid to live without him and afraid to stay involved with him.

How long, Lord? Will you forget me forever? How long will you hide your face from me? 2 How long must I wrestle with my thoughts and day after day have sorrow in my heart? How long will my enemy triumph over me? (Psalm 13: 1-2. NIV)

We were all at Dutch's house, his friend John was sleeping on the couch. John's girlfriend had come over to hang out. We heard a knock at the door. To John's surprise, his wife was at the door yelling and screaming.

Dutch turned to me and said, "Take her to the bedroom and keep her there", referring to the girlfriend. I knew better than to question him. I stood in front of John's girlfriend and attempted to usher her into the bedroom. Somehow, she grabbed a large kitchen knife and began to charge towards John. I was clearly in her path of homicidal intent. She had snapped and planned to kill him or anyone that was in her way. My life was in danger! John became louder and more intense, yelling at her while she was slashing through the air and approaching him. I could hear Dutch saying, "Take that shit somewhere else. I don't need the police coming to my spot!" I had never heard this threatening tone of voice from him. He turned to me and repeated his words, "I said take her to the bedroom!" He was always so gentle with me, but it was clear that he wasn't concerned about me being stabbed to death in a lover's quarrel. He was visibly angry with me, and I could not figure out why. John had chosen his wife and not his girlfriend, sending her into a blind rage. My heart broke for her and me. I could now see that Dutch did not value my life or well-being. I heard the girlfriend growl, "I'm sick of this". Then she dropped the knife and slowly walked to the bedroom door.

I sat in the bedroom with John's girlfriend listening to her muffled cries, barely able to contain my own. I realized that this trap house was a slow descent to hell for anyone who dared to enter. I was not just having a "good time" but making a conscious choice to walk away from God and what He represented. This must have been what the prodigal son felt like in Luke 15:11-32 when he "came to himself". A rich young man walked away from a life of comfort only to end up filthy, broke, and abandoned. I struggled to believe in myself until I realized how little Dutch valued me as a person. I was being buried by all my sin. My needs and wants had built this false self. I was living a life of sin but not because of all the drugs, sex, and partying. But because I had forgotten who I was and who I had been called to be. A child of a Holy God.

The room was a personal shrine to Dutch's dead girlfriend. It definitely had a woman's touch, plenty of pastel colors, ornate theatrical curtains, and decorative pillows. I had never noticed until that instant that we were surrounded by bereavement cards. I had never been concerned about her death until now. What really happened to his girlfriend? How did she die? I knew there was something that seemed different about Dutch, and the mayhem I had just witnessed confirmed a gut feeling. His soft eyes now were hard. This wasn't grief, it was anger. I was soon to learn that this was not going to be an isolated event. In fact, it would be the beginning of his calculated descent into the spirit of murder.

I decided that I was sick of pretending in life. I had managed to live in two contradictory realities. It did not matter how much education I had achieved, or that I had fancy job titles; I was trapped. I was well aware that what had started as casual sex had developed quickly into a serious relationship. I had run from God and refused to acknowledge His authority, which resulted in my brokenness as part of my identity. We both had a change of heart; I was choosing to move on and follow God's plan for my life. Dutch chose revenge through homicide. Leaving an abuser is the most dangerous time for a victim. I had finally decided that I was tired of feeling emotionally drained, manipulated, and deceived. It was time for me to leave. I was going to talk to him about my decision.

We decided to meet at my house. He seemed to be almost giddy. I thought that he was intoxicated. I asked him point-blank, "Are you high?" Dutch then replied, "You got it, don't you?" This was an odd response, even for Dutch. I responded, "What do I have?" With a huge devilish grin on his face, he looked straight through my soul and said, "HIV, I have it. Don't you? I want us to die together." I begin to scream and call on the name of the Lord. He laughed and walked away. "I'll call you later", he said.

I was broken. Bad things happen, but to know that I played a part in my own demise was heartbreaking. I now faced an uncertain future, and I went to get tested for HIV. I also did the only other thing that I knew to do; I prayed. I began to pray for deliverance from sin and acceptance of my fate. I no longer felt trapped. I had now reached a place of spiritual freedom. I believed in Jesus and decided to obey His Word. I knew that I could no longer operate in two worlds. I thought a decision had been made for me by Dutch's deceit, but in reality, God was revealing His grace to me. "Grace," according to the dictionary, is the unmerited favor of God toward mankind.

The Gospel of Jesus Christ teaches that humanity is forgiven through His death on the cross and resurrection. I decided to worship God despite my pending diagnosis and surrender to the will of God for my life. Dutch had issued a death sentence, but God had a different plan. When I arrived at my doctor's appointment, I was completely confident that no matter the results, God was in control. I had learned that we can trust God with the results of our lives. My dangerous collision course of murder and deception would have purpose. If only to serve as a cautionary tale to others. The nurse handed me the envelope. I took a deep breath and opened the envelope and pulled out the results. To my surprise, the results were NEGATIVE. I could no longer live a life of the trap house; I now was going live for Christ in the church house!

Notes On Overcoming:

_____

_____

_____

_____

_____

_____

_____

_____

_____

_____

Notes On Overcoming:

_____

_____

_____

_____

_____

_____

_____

_____

_____

_____

Author Deborah Denise Gibbs

Author Deborah Denise Gibbs

Deborah Denise Gibbs is a first-time author and is a native of Chapel Hill, North Carolina. She is the daughter of Dorothy Mae Bynum and the late Bernice Farrar. She is the mother of four children and the grandmother of eight grandchildren. She is an entrepreneur, the founder of *Sipping Tea Boutique*, and Webcast series on social media.

She attended the Commonwealth District Religious Institute of Richmond, Virginia, and graduated June 13, 2002, with an Associate Degree in Theology. June 10, 2017, she received her bachelor's degree in Theology at Pinnacle Maranatha Bible College of Burlington, North Carolina. Pursuing her knowledge for Christian studies, she graduated May 23, 2021, with a Master of Theology from the University of Alpha and Omega and is currently enrolled at the University of Alpha and Omega of Durham, North Carolina in pursuit of her certification in Christian Counseling.

She accepted the Lord Jesus Christ as her personal savior at the age of ten; was baptized and filled with the gift of the Holy Ghost. She was later ordained as an Evangelist, September 27, 2003. After serving in the ministry from usher to adjutant, she was ordained as a Pastor, June 2, 2012. She is the Senior Pastor of Grace Ministries International of Durham, North Carolina, She's also the founder of Women of Worth Ministries, a ministry that is geared towards empowering men and women in pursuing their God-given purpose. Upon the leading and unction of the Holy Spirit, she flows under a heavy prophetic, healing, and deliverance anointing.

The piercing of trials that she endured, such as rape, molestation, drugs, and domestic violence made her stronger and wiser and helped her to understand her true calling and purpose. Through it all, her relationship with Jesus Christ didn't waver! She is Destined to Win!

To Connect with Author Pastor Deborah Gibbs:
Email: deborahcurtis73@att.net
Website: www.sippingteawithpastord.com/ www.visitgmi.org
Facebook: @Deborah Denise Gibbs

Enough is Enough ~ I'm Done

The morning of October twenty-ninth, two-thousand sixteen at approximately ten fifty in the morning, I received a text message asking me- How are you today? This is where it all began, a simple text that captured my soul. I didn't know the individual, so I didn't respond until later that evening, we didn't have any mutual Facebook friends, so I was like- Why did this individual reach out to me? The young man texted and asked me, "Where is the church located?" I immediately went and checked his Facebook profile and noticed that he wasn't from North Carolina. It was like he knew I had checked his Facebook profile.

Within minutes he responded. He chuckled and said, "Oh, I bet you think I still live in Florida." I laughed and said, "Yes, I was trying to figure it out. Like, why are you asking me where the church is located, and you live in another state?" And we continued to message each other back and forth. Finally, he said, I will be at church on this Sunday coming up." However, he didn't attend Sunday morning worship that following Sunday as he stated. He had been in a car accident before he met me; he said he had taken some medicine and overslept.

Finally, the next Sunday came and we met for the first time, and I was a little nervous. What was interesting was that I'm always nervous before I must speak, but for some reason, it seems like the Holy Spirit showed out, and I mean in a good way. Like, I was astonished at how the Holy Spirit used me in such a way to speak prophetically to him and I had never met him in person before in my life. He was crying like a newborn baby, and he admitted later that everything The Lord said to him through me was true. He asked, "How did you know these things about me, and you never met me before?"

I said, "The Holy Spirit knows all things and I don't know anything except that He reveals to me. I was so nervous. Trust and believe I said what The Holy Spirit instructed me to say without any hesitation or reservation." I was meeting him for the first time, and he was fine, tall, dark, and handsome. I was trying to figure it all out in my mind. "How am I going to preach with a fine specimen of a man looking at me? I'm going to do my best not to look at him."

Well of course it didn't work. I was locking eyes every chance I got. Now, he may not have been looking at me like that, and I know I wasn't looking at him like that, in a sexual manner. Yet, I did think he was cute: beard trimmed goatee style, fine as wine, looking like dark chocolate eye-candy, dressed from head to toe, wearing a brown and white pin-striped Ralph Lauren suit, looking slim and trim, and smelling delicious, Yassss Hunty! I had to overlook him and preach through it all. The Holy Spirit had His way and I praised God that I got through the message. Later that evening the young man texted me. He said, "I really enjoyed the service, and I will be back. I called my mom and told her what happened. I told her about my experience at church and that you didn't know me, but you spoke about some things from my childhood. My mom said it was The Holy Spirit."

So, Wednesday evening comes and it's time for bible study; I was running late. He texts me and asks, "What time does church start? I'm here already." I asked. "What time is it?" He answered, "six-thirty pm." I said, "I'm on my way, but bible study doesn't start until seven-thirty pm." Still recovering from the car accident, he had caught an Uber to bible study on this night. After bible study, I thanked him for coming and I invited him to come back. The young man said, "I really enjoyed the bible study; it was refreshing, and it was what I needed." His Uber driver was on time. As I shook the young man's hand, he asked me, "Can I call you later? I want to share a situation with you. Is that okay?" I said, "Yes, that is fine. But only if you call me before ten pm." He called before ten o'clock. However, he had an unexpected situation.

Apologizing, he asked me, "Can I call you right back?" "Yes, that would be fine." The young man called me back and we talked late into the morning hours! This went on for about a month or so. By now the conversations were more interesting and now I looked forward to having a conversation with him every day. As time went on, we started having dinner at Zaxby's Restaurant, sitting across from each other, gazing into each other's eyes, while having intense conversations about ministry, life, and experiences. We had a lot of things in common, so we got along well, or so I thought. I don't even recall us having a conversation about dating, we just started out having a conversation and we just kept on talking until one night I needed to meet my oldest daughter at the halfway point in South Hill, Virginia. I asked him if he had any plans for the evening and explained that I needed to meet my daughter.

He responded, "No. I don't have any plans." "Would you like to ride with me to South Hill, Virginia to take my oldest grandson to his mom?" I asked. To my surprise, he said, "Yes."

I dropped my grandson off with his mom and my oldest daughter had the chance to meet my young man. For the most part, she liked him. "He's cool and smooth", she said. Indeed, he was. We head back to North Carolina. I don't know what in tarnation made me ask him this question. "So, what are you going to do?" We had come to the agreement that my children were grown and gone. I didn't have any babies at home. Nor did I have to be concerned about the baby-momma-drama with him because his children were with their mom. So basically, I could get married now. "So, what do you want to do?", I asked once again. I had talked with my son about my relationship with this young man. He said, "Mommy, I think that he's cool and could be good for you, but don't rush into anything. Get to know him a little more before you make a final decision."

I went on a consecration and prayed and consulted the Holy Spirit concerning marrying this young man. The response I heard was, "Run!" I thought to myself, "This isn't the Holy Spirit telling me to run. He's a nice guy and I have fallen in love with him. We haven't had sexual intercourse, so my relationship with him isn't based on lust." I received a phone call and a prophet prophesied to me and described my young man to a tee. Now, I had never mentioned anything about a man to this prophet. Yet, the prophet told me that this man was tall, dark, and handsome and was a little thuggish. I was blown away The Holy Spirit still was shouting-" Run!"

Despite the warning, I decided to marry this young man. I choose to do what the prophet said because I believed the prophet who saw me with this man. I knew that the prophet didn't know him, or me for that matter. I had just met the prophet at an award ceremony, so why wouldn't I believe the prophet? The bible says, *Believe His prophets*- 2 Chronicles 20: 20. (KJV)

I was in Mebane North Carolina, getting gas and the young man called me. I answered the phone, and as he began to talk to me something happened to my body; I was losing control of myself, and it was frightening! I went to my mom's house, pulled up in her driveway, and started pleading the blood of Jesus over my body! I called my BFF; she works in the medical field. She told me what was happening. "While speaking to the young man, you opened a doorway," she said. For as long as we had been talking, I hadn't felt my body having an orgasm before, but now I couldn't control them! I had been celibate for six years and I didn't masturbate, nor had I used sex toys. I had been married most of my adult life, so I never had use for a toy. I got off the phone with my BFF and I called the young man back. "Let's meet tonight at Maggiano's for dinner." We met for dinner that night and I broke it off with him. "Let's just be friends", I told him.

Immediately he said. "I've lost my appetite." We left the restaurant, and I didn't talk to him for a while. Eventually, he started back calling me and I fell for his charm and wit once again. I changed my mind about our relationship. On January 10, 2017, we were married. We got married at Grace Ministries International, where I'm currently the Senior Pastor.

Three months into the marriage, we had a dinner engagement with some friends. Everything was going well until I was asked the question, "Did I trust my husband?" I didn't hesitate. I quickly responded, "No!" Well, you could hear a pin drop. My husband was asked the same question, "Did he trust me?" He said, "Yes".

I explained, "We're still getting to know each other. I just met him in October two-thousand sixteen, it's just March two-thousand seventeen." We finished dinner and headed to the car. My husband grabbed my hand and started squeezing my hand so hard. "You are hurting me! Please let my hand go. You are squeezing my hand too hard!"

He opened the car door for me, like the gentleman he could be, and he drove my car with no license, like a bat out hell! My hair was blowing in the wind with the windows up and no air condition, heat, or fan. I thought he was going to turn my ml 350 Mercedes Benz over! He was beyond angry because I had said I didn't trust him. He shouted, "How could you embarrass me like that in front of our friends?"

I apologized to him. We were living with his eighty-five-year-old mother at the time. When we got to the house, I went into the bedroom to get ready for bed. Suddenly, he charged towards me; he started hollering and as he was yelling and hollering, he was spitting in my face. I wanted to vomit; I kept wiping my face. He cussed me out and then falsely imprisoned me, not letting me leave the room. Shocked, I was asking myself, "What in the world is wrong with this lunatic? This is not the person who charmed me!" I tried to run, but there was nowhere to go. You couldn't open the door like a normal door, you had to use a key for the top lock, and I didn't have my key to open the door. As I frantically ran about the room, trying to get away from my husband, he was right on my tail. He was hollering, cussing, and yelling.

I screamed- "Somebody, please help me!" But no one came forth. My husband's aunt was there visiting, but neither she nor my mother-in-law came to help me. My husband pushed me down on the bed and tore my panties off and held me down on the bed. Glaring at me, he said, "Let me get some of this (he said the p-word) before someone else gets it." In his rage, he couldn't even get aroused. That caused him to get even madder and he started hitting me about my head. I tried to cover my face, so he wouldn't blacken my eyes, and thankfully he didn't. The next day we went to the movies as if nothing had happened. I didn't even watch the movie; I was still thinking about the nightmare, and it wasn't on Elm Street!

He apologized. "Baby, I promise it won't happen again." He offered some lame excuse. However, his promise was not kept. His violent temper surfaced over and over again. I left my husband eight times; the ninth time, he put me out. I vowed that the tenth time would be my last. I would be Done!

Nineteen-ninety-three, a movie that came out called, "What's Love Got to Do with It." This movie was about the life of the iconic Tina Turner, and the abuse she tolerated from her husband, Ike Turner for so many years. The abuse ends abruptly one night in the back of a limousine; it is the scene where Ike hits Tina in the mouth. With her mouth bleeding, she looked at Ike, and then she went in for the kill! Tina kicked Ike with all her might and fought him like a warrior! Tina got out of the limousine and ran for her life and didn't look back. Tina got Ike for all the times he put his hands on her. Enough is Enough!

Before the tenth time, about round number eight, we went to Richmond Virginia, my third daughter, who is now a registered nurse, got vested. My husband got lit; he's a functioning alcoholic. He grabbed me, in my face, in with such force that my oldest grandson thought he hit me! I grabbed my keys and pocketbook and took off running; got in my car and left him. Within minutes, I realized, "I'm in Amelia, Virginia and I left my husband with my daughters! What in tarnation was I thinking?" I whipped my car around made a few phone calls to try and figure out where he might be. I found him on the park bench at the Food Lion. He got in the car and started cussing me out. I told him, "You are not going to use that language all the way back to North Carolina. My car is my sanctuary."

I drove down the street a bit, got to the corner, made a right-hand turn as if to head back to North Carolina. Then I stopped the car in the middle of the street. I told my husband, "Get out of my car!" He didn't get out. So, I got out of the car, went to the passenger side, and opened the door. "Get out of my car", I repeated!

I don't know what I was thinking; my husband punched me in my face so hard he knocked me out cold! I don't think I was out that long when I came to, he was standing in front of me swinging his duffle bag at me. I said to myself repeatedly, "Enough is enough, you will not put your hands on me again!" It was pitch black outside except for the convenience store that was open. He took off running towards the store, and I ran in behind him looking for something to use to knock his head off his body. I picked up a bottle of window washer fluid and took off running after him. I was going to use it to strike him.

I heard this voice yelling, "PUT IT BACK!" I realized then the worker thought I was stealing! I dropped the bottle, my husband ran and got in my car, I opened the door of the car and hopped in and held the steering wheel with one hand, and held the door with the other hand. I told my husband, "We are both going to die today!" He put the car in drive and climbed to the other side. I got in his lap with my head laying on the dashboard, and with my black boots on, we went at it! "Enough is enough! You won't ever put yo hands on me again", I said in my Ebonics.

That was what I thought! He tore my face up and I tore his face up! I tried my best to kick his face off. He put his thumb in my mouth and I bit his thumb so hard that I bit it down to the bone. I was so angry and hurt and in shock, I didn't shed not one tear. I was determined to kill him or hurt him badly. He jumped out of the car, I ran him over twice, he wouldn't stay down, he kept popping back up! He went to Pricilla's and was calling somebody on the phone. In the meantime, I made a beeline, headed down the wrong way, looking for him and to see what kind of boulder I could find to bash him in his head.

The police came and told me to get out of the car. My husband had torn off all my clothes, except for my pants, so my chest was exposed. I got out of the car and lifted my hands. One officer asked me what happened. The other officer went to question my husband. The officers made a decision and told me that they should arrest me because he had more blood showing than I did. Then the black officer spoke up, "I can see that your husband is the abusive type. If you get in your car and don't look back, I wouldn't arrest you. If you don't obey, I will arrest us both." Think I didn't get in my car and leave! I left him in Virginia, came back to North Carolina, packed all my things from his mom's house, and left!

One year passed since my husband last hit me. He no longer got so angry. We attempted counseling, and we knew some preacher friends who also ministered to us. We needed the support of others to help steer us in the right direction in order that we would have a successful and lasting marriage. I realized that I wanted more for him than he wanted for himself or us. When he was drinking, he had big dreams for us. When he was sober, I could hardly get two words out of him. When we were dating, we had talked from sunup to sundown.

The morning of November fifteenth two thousand and twenty, the saga began again. I cooked breakfast, while finishing up, my husband told me that he had an interview with Duke Hospital; we were so excited, it was a dream come true for him. He told me about the health benefits, and that he had been looking to put me on his insurance. I told him I had insurance through my job. Well, the conversation went downhill from there. My husband became so angry that he hit me! He began cussing and fussing because having me on his insurance was something he was passionate about. I had pulled the rug from under him. I had planned to leave him by the end of December, twenty-twenty if he didn't stop drinking and smoking. He stopped once and gave his life to Jesus or something. The second time I left, when I came back, he backslid and kept on sliding. I wanted more out of my marriage than those wolf tickets he was selling.

I chose not to leave him this time, only because he wanted to do something different for Thanksgiving, and I keep hearing the Holy Spirit say, "Thanksgiving". I didn't know what was getting ready to happen, but just in case, I prayed and asked The Lord to protect me. I reserved a nice getaway at the Grandover Resort in Greensboro, North Carolina, and the Ritz Carlton in Atlanta, Georgia. I spent over five thousand dollars on our Thanksgiving get-away, and I couldn't get my money back. Therefore, I chose to stick it out until then. He came home early Sunday night, picking at me. He asked me, "Why don't you leave?" He then took the pillow and tried to suffocate me. He had been drinking. Finally, he left me alone.

Moving forward, on Thanksgiving eve we prepared to go on our getaway. I called my husband to let him know, the Grandover Resort had called me and stated that we had to check in before 11:00 pm. My husband got off work at 11:30 pm and we would've had to check-in on Thanksgiving Day instead of Thanksgiving eve which was Wednesday night. I made it to the house, and I noticed that my husband seemed a little different, I knew he had been drinking, but he didn't seem as happy like something was either bothering him or something was on his mind. We're finally on our way, nice drive down, get to the Resort, get unpacked, get settled in, and I mean *settled in.* Yassss Hunty, that part!

The next morning, we went to our breakfast reservation at the Grandover. My husband coughs and I said, "Covid?" My comment made him mad as FIRE! He didn't eat his food, we got up and left. We walked around the resort, talked, and took selfies. Then we went to our room and got changed. My husband went downstairs to get a drink and smoke a cigarette. I came downstairs and asked him to do a Facebook live with me and he agreed even though he didn't really like doing them, but I had to wait until he finished smoking. I didn't want to wait that long, so I did the live without him. My phone went dead, so I went to the room to charge my phone. My husband wanted to go and get something to eat; we went downstairs and as we walked towards the car in the parking lot and proceeded to get in the car, my husband said something petty to me.

My response to him was, "You found time to find a drink." My remark was a trigger. He threw his phone down to the ground and charged towards me like a bat out of hell. He choked me with all his might. He said, "Bitch, I will kill you with my bare hands!" I told him, just above a whisper, "Take your hands off my neck!" He let me go. I asked him, "Where do you want to eat?" We drove around and got lost. Frustrated, he decided that he didn't want anything to eat; he wanted to go home. It was an answered prayer! We finally got back to the Resort, and he was so angry. He assaulted me again in the room, blaming me for us getting lost, the argument, him having a bad time; everything was my fault. He packed his things and we left. He cussed me out a whole hour, all the way back to Durham, North Carolina. Once we arrived back home, he threw me the keys. I went back to the Resort, called my BFF in Virginia, she prayed for me, and I went to bed and cried myself to sleep.

I woke up the next morning to the police and Chief of Security knocking on my resort door. They had viewed the videotape and the police pressed charges against my husband for assault on a female. The judge issued an emergency restraining order against my husband!

On September 15, 2021, we went to court, my husband's lawyer responded to the charges- he plead guilty to assault on a female. The Judge asked me did I want to have any words. My remarks were, *"I love my husband, I'm sorry our marriage didn't work out and I forgive him."* My husband then tried to plead his side to the Judge. The Judge wasn't having it and told my husband, *"I know why you assaulted your wife because she was leaving you and you wanted to stop her from leaving."* My husband quickly said that I had the keys. The Judge reprimanded him for talking while the Judge was making his remarks and demanded the bailer to take him into custody. The judge was so upset and stated, *"I don't know where you're from but here, in Guilford County, we don't condone a man putting his hands on a female!"* The Judge asked me did I want to add to his judgment and I replied that he needed to go to jail because he hasn't learned his lesson. The Judge inquired more regarding his record and the DA went all the way back to 2011 and his record was pretty thick: assault on a female, DUI'S, and a DPO.

That was it! The Judge didn't want to hear anymore. He sentenced my husband to thirty days suspended sentence, seven active days in jail, eighteen months supervised probation, plus all fees, and domestic violence class. Upon leaving the courtroom, the Judge told me that he was glad that I didn't die. I thanked him for the Victory! My prayer was answered. God's will was done on my behalf in Jesus' name. ***Enough is Enough***!

The piercing of trials made me understand my purpose. I am a vessel that the Lord can use to minister and pray for women that have and are dealing with domestic violence. I want women that are suffering in silence to know that you don't have to. You have a voice! I learned that it's vital to obey the Holy Spirit's leading. God will not lead you astray. Don't allow your situation to stop you from getting the help you may need; it could very well save your life. October 2021 was domestic violence month; October 21, 2021, featured Sipping Tea with Pastor D webcast in dedication to domestic violence survivors. I'm currently moving forward with my life, seeking wise counsel, and have consulted my lawyer, to move forward with the divorce decree. I'm excited about my next chapter and what new endeavors await me! While having endured false imprisonment, sexual abuse, physical abuse, and mental abuse, I know it was only by the Grace of God that I'm not demised. I'm a survivor of domestic violence that was abused and used for someone else's breakthrough. *Pierced for Purpose*, I'm *Destined to Win*!

Notes On Overcoming:

Notes On Overcoming:

_____

_____

_____

_____

_____

_____

_____

_____

_____

_____

_____

++Dr. Rhonda Royal Hatton

++Dr. Rhonda Royal Hatton

++Dr. Rhonda Royal Hatton is a pastor, missionary, actress, playwright, director, poet, storyteller, inspirational speaker, teacher, author and entrepreneur. A prophet in her own right, she is the oldest of five children. Rhonda was born to the late Ulysses Royal Jr. and Mother Evangelist Brenda Best Royal Warren. Born and raised in Camden, New Jersey, Rhonda gave her life to the Lord at fourteen years old. Preaching her initial sermon at sixteen years old, she served as a youth leader and junior evangelist. Rhonda founded the theater group, *Gifts of God*. They traveled the South Jersey and Philadelphia area performing- "Intoxication: Don't Get High: Give Jesus A Try!", a play focused on saying "no" to drug abuse and domestic violence. Rhonda is an award-winning orator and spoken word artist. She co-founded and facilitated an open mic, *Living Words*, for six years as an evangelistic outreach endeavor during her tenure as an Outreach Minister.

Rhonda has published two books of poetry and dramatic presentations, *Revelations: A Book of Ministerial Monologues* and *Prophetic Poetry and Sanctuary: A Book of Inspirational Writings and Prophetic Poetry*. She is also an author in the collaborative work, *Destined 2 Win* Book series. Rhonda is the founder and artistic director of A Royal Priesthood Performing Arts, Inc., a 501 (c) 3 nonprofit performing arts foundation.

Rhonda attended North Carolina Central University and earned her B.A. in Theater Education. She has served as a high school drama teacher and fourth grade elementary school teacher. She has also served as the Lutheran Campus Minister to NCCU. Rhonda acquired her Masters of Church Ministry degree from Duke Divinity School in 2007 and her Doctorate of Theology from Bible Institutes of America Theological Seminary in 2016. She was affirmed to the five-fold ministry office of Apostle in August of 2017.

Rev. Dr. Rhonda Royal Hatton is the founder and senior pastor of Celebration Ministries, Lutheran Church in Durham, NC. She is also the founder and Presider of Royal Priesthood Fellowship of Churches.

Apostle Hatton is the spiritual mentor to many pastors and leaders. She is the Overseer for two churches and three para-ministries. She has been married for 28 years to Bishop–Elect Pastor Ian Hatton and they have two beautiful daughters.

To connect with Dr. Hatton
Facebook: @Rhonda Royal Hatton
Email: hattonrhonda@gmail.com

Mental Health in The Church:
It's Not Always a Demon-Dispelling the Stigma

We, in the church, acknowledge that all human brokenness is the result of sin infecting the human condition at the fall. Humanness and spirituality have always had a conflict because the flesh of humans can blind them to the manifestations of the spiritual world. There is a scripture where the Apostle Paul writes, "*I know a man in Christ who fourteen years ago, whether in the body I do not know, or whether out of the body I do not know, God knows, such a one was caught up to the third heaven. And I know such a man, whether in the body or out of the body I do not know, God knows.*" 2 Corinthians 12:2-3 And the Truth of the matter is that God does know but we as humans don't always know because of the intertwining of both realms natural and spiritual. And because of this, we can diagnose a condition that is a human condition as a spiritual one, when in case it is just a flaw because of the Fall.

In this writing, I am going to address a subject that is faced with much ignorance and stigma especially in the church world and particularly in the African-American church community. In many spiritual communities, this subject is treated as taboo. The subject I am speaking of is mental illness. There is a lot of confusion surrounding mental illness and because of that, many in the church have not, do not, and/or will not get the help that they need. This is a complex subject and because of people's misunderstanding and even shame. Many in the body of Christ suffer in silence. Many people have gone undiagnosed and have negatively affected relationships in their churches, workplaces, communities, and families because of the stigma that surrounds mental illness.

It is clearly seen, in some cases, that there are people in the church, even leaders, that clearly have personality disorders, suffer from depression, bipolarism, and/ or paranoia but refuse to see someone to assist them with getting their mental state healthy. They become super-spiritual if it is addressed and begin to rebuke demons, devils, and all evil entities but the truth be told, it is not always a demon. Some people, in the church, are suffering from mental illness, which could have been caused by an in balance in the brain. Do not get me wrong, I wholly believe in casting out demons, devils, and the like, but we as leaders in the body of Christ must be most discerning in these cases if we are going to encourage healing. First and foremost, we must not be in denial and we must evaluate our own mental health. Whether the disorder is brought on by the stress of traumatic experiences, or a genetic situation, mental illness is real and needs to be dealt with effectively in our spiritual communities, so that the church can compassionately support those dealing with it.

Misunderstanding and rejection of the sick are not uncommon. In biblical times, there were many who suffered from various diseases, like leprosy, barrenness, blindness, lameness, blood issues, palsies, mental illness, and the like. In the ninth chapter of John's Gospel, we can see Jesus of Nazareth, confronting a community's attitude toward its sick, while at the same time healing people in their midst. He's a master at that. In this instance, He heals two kinds of blindness. First, he gives physical sight to a blind man. And second, an important miracle happens as he exposes and begins to heal the blinding darkness of stigma. In Jesus' day, illnesses were often attributed to sin. So the disciples' question was not, "How did this happen?" because they thought they had already figured that out. They were sure the cause was sin. They just wanted Jesus to help them ascribe blame to the right party. Their question was, *"Who sinned, this man or his parents?"* Jesus would have none of it. *"You are asking the wrong question,"* he responded. He knew the question arose from wrong assumptions—presumptions based on ignorance and stigma.

Some mental disease is caused by spiritual issues or demonic oppression, but we also have to accept that it's not always a demon. I do recognize and believe in the evil in this world and the world beyond, but in dealing with mental illnesses, we in the church must understand that some people's issues are due to chemical imbalance or brain disease. It is no different than if one had an organ disease in the body and were experiencing adverse effects because of it. In dealing with this issue in the church, I often ask people if their heart was skipping a beat and the doctor suggested a medication that would help it function normally, would you not take it? Of course you would, full of faith and all. You would believe God that with prayer and medicine your healing was on the way. So, why do we make people feel that their faith lacks if they have to take medicine for their brain? It is an organ, is it not? Mental illnesses are medical conditions. They are disorders of the brain.

Like the diabetic who has a malfunctioning pancreas or the person whose autoimmune system has failed, those with mental illnesses have a part of their physical bodies that isn't working as it should. Like other ailments that have no known cure, there is no cure for many kinds of mental illnesses, except by way of a miracle. Those of us, in the Faith community, believe in miracles. Mental illness can be chronic and debilitating, however, like other medical conditions, with the right medical treatments and support from loved ones and the community, mental illnesses can be managed and individuals can live meaningful lives.

Let us think of all the functions our brains perform! When some parts of the brain aren't able to do some of those things, then the ways we think, how we feel and express emotions, and even our ability to relate to others and perform daily functions can be severely disrupted. Like other parts of our bodies, the brain is *fearfully and wonderfully made* - an incredibly complex creation of our God, our mainframe that controls our bodies externally and internally. Depending on which section is malfunctioning and what kind of brain chemicals are behaving badly, mental illnesses manifest in different ways. So, there are lots of different diagnoses and labels used to describe various mental illnesses, including: depression, schizophrenia, bipolar, obsessive–compulsive disorder (OCD), post-traumatic stress disorder (PTSD), and others. Some of these are caused by our exposure to traumatic events, in our childhood or adulthood. Some are caused by recreational drug use or abuse. Remember the commercial, this is your brain on drugs, with the frying egg? Some of these are caused by our experiences spiritual in nature, something evil has entered in because of spiritual doors that have been opened. Our brain is so complex that it will respond to these stimuli by going into preservation or protection mode thus causing parts of us to protect other parts of us. Some illnesses, we are simply born with and may not realize it, as a baby, but as we grow symptoms begin to present themselves.

Know that this disease has no respect of persons, it impacts the young, old, poor, affluent, less educated and highly educated, men and women—touching lives in all nations, races, and religions. Mental illness is also widespread throughout society. In fact, in the United States, it is estimated that 60 million Americans (1 in 17) are living with a mental illness, which is more than twice the number who live with diabetes (25.8 million); nearly 5x the number dealing with cancer (13 million); and about 60x those diagnosed with HIV/Aids (1.1 million). About every 15 minutes, someone with severe depression takes his or her own life. With those kinds of numbers, it is likely that 1 in 4 adults will experience a mental health disorder in a given year. Often people with mental illnesses turn to drugs and alcohol to try to address their mental anguish. Many cannot hold steady employment and thus those with mental illnesses make up over 25% of the homeless population in the U.S. It is also estimated that about 20-25% of jail and prison inmates, as well as youth involved with juvenile justice, live with a mental illness. There is an even great number of people who are undiagnosed. They are in our communities, our neighborhoods, our families, and our churches.

When we have encountered congregants who have mental challenges, perhaps they are moody, unstable, can't keep a job, or a place to live, commonly make rash or foolish decisions, all their personal relationships are volatile, they are unusually paranoid, they operate in the spirit of offense all the time, down and or depressed frequently, suicidal, violent, and/or they display behaviors that make you uncomfortable or question their character. Many of us, in the church, have dismissed it as them just *acting out* or wanting attention. How many of us have joked about people saying, "They must have not had their medicine today" or you know Sister So and So is *CrayCray*, or Brother Such and Such is Looney Tunes. As leaders in the church, we have to recognize that it is not a joking or funny matter but a serious one and it is our duty to work to break the stigma that, "all you need is Jesus." Yes, we do need Jesus and we do need prayer and some need deliverance but many need counseling, and/or medication therapy.

In my own experiences, I have seen that various communities have responded to those with mental illnesses with ignorance and stigma. In the African American community, we have seen people shamed and people ashamed that someone in their family needs mental health care. Many have shied away from getting the care that they need because of perpetrated stigma. Many have shied away from the church because when it comes to their mental illnesses they are disgraced for "not wanting to be delivered" and/or "not having enough faith to be healed", when what they really need to do is see a natural doctor along with counseling from their spiritual advisor.

Contrary to some popular beliefs, in the faith community, Jesus believes in doctors. The Apostle Luke was a physician and if you study the miraculous healing in scripture you will find that the afflicted persons had spent all their money on the doctors but their situation was one where they needed doctor Jesus, who is referred to as the Great Physician. Jesus responded differently to persons suffering from diseases. He never condemned people for being sick. In the scripture, the blind man's family was treated with suspicion and blame but Jesus took another approach, Jesus reminds us that we should care for those society has given up on, such as the naked, the hungry, the imprisoned, and the sick.

So, how should we respond to people with illnesses in their brains? As with all Kingdom love, we should respond first out of the right heart, then with the right ideas, and finally with the right actions. Once our ignorance is addressed and our compassion is ignited, there are some practical ways a church can help overcome stigma and be a place of healing to the mentally ill and their families. Then persons, including church leaders, who struggle in this area will feel free to pursue help and not feel so alone and ashamed that they may resort to drastic measures.

Here are some ideas:

A. First and foremost, we must destigmatize those who suffer from mental illness by not demonizing the disease. We have to make our churches a safe place for those that have mental illnesses and are battling to combat it. To do that, a church body needs to be transparent about brokenness and acknowledge that all of us struggle with weak areas in our lives. *"For all have sinned and fall short of the glory of God," Romans 3:23*

B. Secondly, we must equip our churches with the tools it needs to serve those with mental illnesses and their families. We must identify our congregation's theology of suffering. We have to train our clergy and staff, offer support groups, create alliances with local mental health agencies, and health professionals.

C. Include them in our spiritual gatherings. Invite them in. We must treat hurting people like people, not like the plague. Be friendly. Don't overlook or pass them on to others, but at the same time, set healthy boundaries. Don't expect them to be able to do that, so guiding them appropriately is in order.

D. We must address the stigma of mental illness by talking about it openly. Include general prayers for the mentally ill in congregational praying. Highlight and support local ministries that serve the homeless, the incarcerated, and indigent mentally ill populations.

E. We must treat those with mental illnesses and their families as you would any who have chronic pain in their lives or are lifelong caregivers. Pray for and with them. Give them space to talk about what is going on in their lives. As needed, refer them to professional help.

F. Attend, when we can, to practical needs such as transportation to medical appointments, assist, when appropriate, with extraordinary expenses or refer them to resources that can provide that service. We must do our research because this population is a part of our churches whether big or small.

In the story of the blind man, what if the community had not been so concerned with assigning blame, but instead had been consumed in administering love? What if their question, instead of, "Who sinned?" was, "How can we help?" Perhaps instead of investigating the healing, they would have been participating in it. Going forward, let us not dismiss people to simply demonic activity when they need spiritual and natural applications.

Mother Teresa showed us how to love this way through her life and in her prayers:

"Dearest Lord,

May I see you today and every day in the person of your sick, and while nursing them, minister to you. Though you hide yourself behind the unattractive disguise of the irritable, the exacting, the unreasonable, may I still recognize you and say, 'Jesus, my patient, how sweet it is to serve you.' "

Resources for those with mental illnesses and their families:

National Alliance on Mental Illness (NAMI) http://www.nami.org

Mental Health Grace Alliance http://mentalhealthgracealliance.org/

Video and Audio Sessions on "Mental Health and the Church" Sponsored by Saddleback Church (Rick Warren) http://www.youtube.com/watch?v=2K5-5DV1sv4

Books:

Grace for the Afflicted: A Clinical and Biblical Perspective on Mental Illness, Matthew S. Stanford, IVP Books

Troubled Minds: Mental Illness and the Church's Mission, Amy Simpson, IVP Books

Notes On Overcoming:

_____

_____

_____

_____

_____

_____

_____

_____

_____

Notes On Overcoming:

_____

_____

_____

_____

_____

_____

_____

_____

_____

_____

Author Erica Wilder

Author Erica Wilder

Minister Erica Wilder was born and raised in Lawrence, Massachusetts, a city on the Merrimack River in the state's northeast corner. Her family moved in 1988 to neighboring North Andover, Massachusetts. She now lives in Boston, Massachusetts, where she is raising her musically gifted son, Jordan. Since 1991, when she gave her life to Christ, she has been an active member of the historic, Calvary Baptist Church in Haverhill. It was there that she was licensed to preach in February of 2013, under the late Reverend Dr. Gregory E. Thomas, and has served on the Usher Board, Teller Committee, Delegate Committee and is part of the M'kaddesh Liturgical Dance Ministry and sings with various choirs. She is an active participant in the United Baptist Convention of Massachusetts, Rhode Island, and New Hampshire, and is a part of the United Baptist Convention Music Ministry. She is the dean of the UBC Congress.

Since relocating to Boston, Massachusetts, Minister Wilder is now a member of Timothy Baptist Church under the leadership of Rev. Dr. Larry Green Sr. She is pursuing a diploma in Urban Studies from Gordon Conwell Theological Seminary in Boston, Massachusetts, and later plans to pursue a Master of Divinity degree. Minister Erica Wilder is a child of the Most-High God. She says- *"I love the Lord because He first loved me. He has seen me through so many things, and I just want to serve Him with my whole heart. I am humbled, blessed, and grateful to God for the opportunity to do His will."*

Contact Author Erica Wilder:
Email: faithanew04@gmail.com
Facebook: @faithanew04
Snapchat: @nubianqueen2816
Instagram: @erykah78

Hidden in Plain Sight

Do you ever feel like your work goes unnoticed? Do you ever feel as though you are just existing, in ministry, on your job, or in life? Well, this chapter is for you. In this chapter, I want to talk about hiding in plain sight. I want to share my challenges in going forward in ministry and in life, but I also want to share with you my struggles within myself, as a minister of the gospel, and as an overcomer of adversity. I want to conclude the chapter by stressing the importance of being obedient to do the things that God is calling us to do. I pray that this chapter will encourage the hearts and minds of men and women alike who are struggling in ministry and struggling in other areas of their lives.

Oftentimes we are so hard on ourselves, and we deem ourselves unworthy. How many of you know that sometimes we become our own worst critics? There are times when we can be so hard on ourselves; focused only on our weaknesses and ignoring our strengths. Or perhaps it's just me, I know I tend to be hard on myself. But I want to challenge us to change our mindset. God wants to do a new thing in our lives and for him to do that new thing in our lives, we must change our thinking. We must change our mindset. The word of God tells us that *we are more than conquerors through Him that loved us.* Romans 8: 37 (NIV). The word also tells us-*let God transform us into a new person by changing the way we think. Then you will learn to know God's will for you, which is good and pleasing and perfect.* Romans 12:2 (NLT) I want to encourage you and remind you that what God has for you, is indeed for you. It may not come at the time that we think it should come but it will, indeed, come! *Delayed is not denied!*

So, let me tell you a little bit about myself. I was licensed to preach in February of 2013, by the late Dr. Reverend Gregory E. Thomas, of Calvary Baptist Church in Haverhill, Massachusetts. I have always been a quiet person until God called me to preach. I was like Moses. I declared, "I can't speak in front of people!" However, God had other plans. So, I completed a program titled- *Call and Response.* This program was designed for those who felt that they were called to preach. The program included instructional sessions and follow-up assignments. Out of 17 people enrolled, we ended up having seven that completed the entire process. I was the third person to get licensed out of this program. After I got licensed, my pastor told me, "You're going to be one of the busier ministers that we have." I remember saying to myself, "I am the quiet preacher. I don't think so!"

But God knew what He was doing, and He had given a glimpse of what He was going to do with my ministry to my pastor, the late Rev. Dr. Gregory E. Thomas. I received many opportunities to preach in various churches. My first outside preaching engagement was at New Hope Baptist Church in Portsmouth, New Hampshire where the pastor was the late Rev. Dr. Arthur Hillson. After Rev. Thomas passed away, Rev. Hillson took me under his wing, and he became my mentor and friend. Rev. Hilson invited me to preach on the closing night of his revival! It was a privilege and awesome experience, to say the least; to God be the glory! After that Rev. Hilson showed me how to officially accept a preaching engagement when I was afforded the opportunity to preach at New Fellowship Baptist Church in Nashua, New Hampshire where the pastor was the late Rev. Dr. Bertha Perkins. As the Lord saw fit, I was afforded many opportunities to preach to various churches, First Baptist Church in Saugus, Massachusetts, Emmanuel Baptist Church in Malden, Massachusetts, and Third Baptist Church in Lawrence, Massachusetts, just to name a few. God gave me the platforms to preach, and for that, I am most grateful.

The word of God tells us, *"A prophet is honored everywhere except in his own hometown and among his relatives and his own family."* Mark 6: 4 (NLT). Before I left Calvary Baptist Church, I tried to and be a blessing to them; I tried to assist while we were without a pastor, and I did have the opportunity to preach many Sundays as pulpit supply. For that I'm grateful, but my growth was being stunted there. After 26 years at Calvary Baptist Church, God decided to move me somewhere else. He brought me to Timothy Baptist Church in Roxbury, Massachusetts, where the pastor is the Rev. Dr. Larry Green Sr. It was here that God blessed me and allowed me to grow.

I am blessed and fortunate to preach every third and fifth Sunday. I also work in the Media Ministry, was a Superintendent for a while, and hold a position on the Advisory Board. It was here at Timothy Baptist Church that I was able to grow in my preaching ministry. At my former church, we had a very short time frame for how long we could preach. If you went over the length of time, you were the topic of the next minister's meeting. So, the first time that I preached at Timothy, I asked the pastor what the time frame for a sermon was, and it was nearly double what we were able to preach at my former church. So, that, in turn, required me to do more research and to study more deeply to be sure that I was creating an effective message for the extended time frame.

I'm grateful and thankful for the opportunities that I have been afforded at Timothy Baptist Church. Yet, there are struggles that I have had. This is in no way a bashing of my pastor because I love him dearly. However, because we are talking about being **pierced for a purpose**, it allows me to share some transparent moments with you.

Oftentimes women are overlooked in ministry, and not just in ministry, but even in corporate settings. There have been various positions on my job for which I have been overlooked. Often, you find that the males are the ones who are getting more promotions, and the males are the ones that are making more money, right? There is a familiar passage in scripture that oftentimes gets misconstrued, for it says- *women should be silent during the church meetings. It is not proper for them to speak. They should be submissive, just as the law says.* Corinthians 14:34. But let me ask you this, who was the first person who found Jesus' clothes laid out in the borrowed tomb and went to proclaim the good news that indeed, our savior has risen? It was a woman! Ministry and the pastorate have always been a male-dominated field and depending on the association your church is with, delegates more than you know or realize, are mostly males.

There have been times when I felt like, "God, what am I doing here? What else am I supposed to be doing, Lord? Why aren't things moving in a different direction? Am I missing something, Lord? Perhaps you have felt that way sometimes. In our flesh, we struggle because we know what God has called us to do, but we do not understand His timing. God's timing is not our timing, and those things He wants to do in our lives require preparation; in our lives, and in the lives of those around us. If the truth be told, a recent event caused me to think about God's timing and my feelings about the event. Someone got ordained, and in my flesh, I felt slighted. Because here it is that I'm doing all that the Lord has called me to do-preaching, teaching, singing, dancing, studying to show myself approved and being in school. Yet somehow it seems like I was not even thought about, I am not even on a track towards ordination. And I wrestled with that. Don't get me wrong, I don't have a problem with the person who did get ordained, but it just felt like a slap in the face. And then I was speaking to someone, and they reminded me that many people, including those at my church, may not even know of my other roles. On Saturday mornings I am on a Christian radio station, and I am a co-producer of the Gospel Connection International. We come on the radio station 104.9 on Saturday morning from 6 to 10 am Eastern Standard Time, and we play gospel music, discuss local artists, and what they're doing, and we also promote services, events, and books that are relevant to the community that we serve. On Sundays, we have another producer, and his name is Marc Stallworth. I was talking with Marc, and I shared with him my feelings about my challenges in the ministry, and the Lord used Marc to speak to me and to speak to my spirit. The Lord gave these words to Marc for me, and I want to share them with you today. It has only been confirmed, he kept calling me Bishop.

Marc said, "It has only been confirmed! Elevation is definitely on your path, and you are on a collision with greatness! But God! I have seen where God is getting ready to elevate you to the next level, and all I can say is- be ready!"

God has been speaking to me for a while now, and it seems as though I'm on the break of something great; that I'm on the break of my breakthrough! God is using people in my life to encourage me and to help me get to where He wants to bring me. When Marc said that I was on a collision course with greatness, that resonated with me. I say all this to say, that when it is indeed your time that God will open the doors for you. If God had given me the positions or appointments that I thought I deserved, when I wanted them, I probably would have messed things up. I would have messed up the blessings that God had in store for me. Now, God is encouraging me to walk through doors that He alone has opened for me because now it is my time. God is telling you to walk through those doors that He alone has opened for you, as well. I encourage you to walk through those doors that no man can close. When God opens the door for you all you need to do is step out on faith and walk through that window of opportunity, walk through that door and do that thing that God has placed inside your heart. Your time is now! You are no longer that person who is hiding in plain sight. God has seen your tears, and He has heard your pain. He has heard your cries and wants you to know that *delayed is not denied.*

When you remain humble you do not have to do anything, because God is the one who is going to elevate you. You will no longer be hidden in plain sight. Perhaps you were hidden in plain sight because it's not your time yet. Just like in the book of Ruth, we find that Esther had an appointed time in which she was to be elevated into her purpose and into the plan that God had for her. No matter how hard it may be, no matter how frustrating you may get, just know that God sees you. He is preparing you for such a time as this. Know that if God were to give it to you any time before the appointed time, you would not be able to handle where it is that God is about to take you! We each have our own crosses to bear, and your journey is not like my journey. God is doing some things in me, and He is doing some things in you. Get ready! Get ready! Get ready! God is taking you and me to higher heights and deeper depths.

Oftentimes, I've heard that perhaps my ministry is not that I am going to be the pastor of a particular church; perhaps the ministry God has for me is something that's far beyond the four walls of a church building. I hear the Lord say, "I am elevating you to a new level, one that you can't even fathom or even imagine." What God has for me is greater than I can even imagine or think.

So, it's not that God has hidden you, He is preparing you! God has you and He has me in a place of preparation so that we can go forth and do ministry. God is expanding the borders! He is enlarging your territory and He is enlarging my territory. God is up to something! I may not understand it, but God is doing something great, not just in me but in each of you as well. I know beyond a shadow of a doubt, that I was *pierced for a purpose.*

God makes no mistakes, only greatness. I know that if I stay true to Him, and remain humble, God will take me from being hidden in plain sight to the limelight. He can do that for you, too! Know that because you have been *Pierced for a Purpose,* you too, are *Destined to Win*!!!

Notes On Overcoming:

_____

_____

_____

_____

_____

_____

_____

_____

_____

Notes On Overcoming:

_____

_____

_____

_____

_____

_____

_____

_____

_____

_____

Author Harriet Holder

Author Harriet Holder

Harriet Holder was born in Barbados on August 20, 1959, and entered the United States of America on November 19, 1971, to live with her mother and four other siblings. In the early '70s, The United States of America was going through segregation and in 1973 had to endure the busing era for three more years in the Boston School System.

Harriet graduated from Boston High School in 1977 and went on to attend Boston Business School to receive an Executive Secretarial Certificate. After graduation, she got a job as a secretary for a banking officer at the Bank of New England in Boston, Massachusetts in 1981. In 1985, she married her husband, Sven Holder. During the five-year marriage, they had a beautiful daughter, named Nichole Holder in 1987.

The pain of surviving the busing era caused Harriet not to attend college, but later in her 40's in 2008, She was able to receive a master's degree in Business Administration from Eastern Nazarene College in Quincy, Massachusetts.

During the late 90s, she became a member of the Grace Church of All Nations, under the leadership of Bishop Foxworth. In 1997 she became an Elder. Harriet has been a leader for thirty-one years, serving the Dorchester community. She joined the World Evangelism Mission Team and went with them on her first missionary journey to Manitoba, Canada. She started her own ministry in 2000 and through this ministry, she did her second mission journey to Barbados. In 2016, she went on to serve as an Associate Minister under the leadership of Pastor George Arabor, of Fountain of Grace in Canton, Massachusetts.

Harriet worked as a night auditor, a floral designer, and a wedding consultant in Westwood, Massachusetts. She started an event planner business named, *Dreams Do Come True Company*. In 2018, Harriet decided to go back to school to get a master's degree in Mental Health at Cambridge College in Charlestown, Massachusetts. She achieved the degree in 2021. She is presently working at T Jocelyne Counseling and Clinic in Brockton, Massachusetts as a Master-Level Family Therapist serving couples and families.

Currently, Harriet is working on her own ministry, named Liberty International Ministries, where she will be doing teaching, deliverance, and assisting churches in any capacity that is being led by the Holy Spirit.

Contact Author Harriet Holder:
Email: harrietholder883@gmail.com
Facebook: @harriet.holder.9

Almost Went to Prison, but was Called to the Pulpit

"You intended to harm me, but God intended it for good to accomplish what is now being done" Genesis 50:20

When I was growing up, I always said to my family that I was going to get married at 25 years old. I got married on August 31, 1985, right after my 25th birthday. I knew my husband when I was about six years old on the Island of Barbados when I was visiting his family. I am not sure when he came to the United States, but I came to Boston on November 19, 1971, and he went to New York. I met him again in New York when I was a teenager at, 16 years old, and we kept in touch. I started dating him in 1983, two years prior to our marriage in August of 1985. After two years of marriage in 1987, we had a beautiful daughter, who we named, Nichole Yvette. I was 27 years old when Nichole was born. My husband and I had a savings account of $30,000.00. In March of 1988, we purchased a three-bedroom townhouse in Dorchester, Massachusetts. I had started working at the Bank of New England in 1981, prior to getting married, and was promoted to a new position in 1985. We purchased a brand-new Toyota Corolla car. We keep acquiring things, but my life started getting worse instead of better in my marriage.

I remember when I was having a conversation with my husband about buying a washing machine and dryer. I noticed that he was getting upset when I said that I never went to a laundromat. This was when I was first introduced to domestic violence, with my husband trying to get his hands around my throat. After all was said and done, he apologized, and we made up. Domestic violence became the elephant in the room for our marriage. We never discussed that night, but it was hanging over our heads like a dark cloud. We acquire things fast, but we did not have a vision or a purpose for our lives. This caused our relationship to lose the love and the purpose that we started out with for each other. *"For the plans I have for you are good and to give you an expected end."* Jeremiah 29:11 (KJV). I did not know that God was going to use the good, the bad, and the ugly to work out his plans for my life.

I was depressed and was very unhappy. One weekend my husband went to New York, but I did not know that I had an appointment with the Holy Spirit. First, I did not know about the Holy Spirit even though I was raised in the church. When I was raised in our church, we were taught about the Father and about Jesus the Christ, but we were not taught about the Holy Spirit or the third party of the Godhead. I was in my house by myself when I heard someone talking to me. I heard, "You knew me when you were a child, but I want you to know me as an adult". I said, "Know who?" Then I heard someone say, "My name is Parakletos".

I had to get the dictionary to find the meaning, and it means the Holy Spirit or the Holy Ghost. Something broke inside of me, and I started crying and speaking in a language that I did not know. I came from an Island that only speaks English, but out of my mouth was this foreign dialect that I did not recognize. I covered my mouth, but I heard this voice say, "Take your hand from your mouth." I slowly took my hand from my mouth, and out came this language that kept coming. The more it came, the better it sounded. My body started feeling lighter like I had not a care in the world. I had a sweet fellowship with the Holy Spirit on that Saturday. We sang hymns from my childhood that I have forgotten and scriptures that I had learned came out from my belly, and I had a time with my new friend. Words cannot explain how I felt after carrying burdens for so long, and now no burdens could be felt on my back.

It seemed that when I fellowshipped with my new friend, the Holy Spirit, he took everything away from me that was bothering me, burdening me, or making me unhappy. In its place, he gave me a peace as described in the scripture -*And the peace of God, which passeth all understanding, shall keep your hearts and minds through Christ Jesus.* (Philippians 4:7 KJV). When my husband came home, he came back to a changed woman, but he did not know it, nor did I know it. I had had an encounter with the Holy Spirit! I wanted to know who this person was, so I started going to church with my husband. He was already going to a Pentecostal Church, but I had said to him previously that I was not going until I was ready. It was not that I was ready, God was ready for me. I looked back and realized it was my appointed time. It was my hour of visitation with God to change the trajectory of my life at thirty years old. God had waited for me all this time and stopped me in my tracks from going in another direction that would have caused me to end up in Framingham Maximum Prison for the rest of my life.

And we know that in all things God works for the good of those who love him, who have been called according to his purpose. (Romans 8:28 NIV). I did not know that I had a calling on my life; nor did I know about gifts that I was born with. I came to this knowledge of what was inside me through brokenness. God knew what he placed inside of me, and he needed a conduit to get it out on display. He knew that domestic abuse was going to be the instrument that caused me to be broken open. God used it for His good to get what he placed inside me to come to its fullness. He worked the situation for His good because he knew my purpose in Him.

Prior to going to church, we were having huge arguments that turned into ongoing domestic abuse. I got sick of being tired; I was not happy with my marriage. We did not communicate well, which caused a lot of heated conversations about overspending, and the marriage started falling apart. To put more pressure on a bad situation, I lost my job at the bank. I wanted a way out, and the only thing that I could see to put the end to my misery was to kill my husband. I have an analytical and calculating mind, so I first planned it out in my head, then I was ready to do it.

It was around that time The City of Boston was having the highest murder rate because women were fed up with their mates beating them. The women killed their spouses but ended up at Framingham Maximum Prison. Governor Michael Dukakis was in office at that time, and some of the women claimed that they killed their spouses in self-defense. He pardoned a lot of them, but some of them are still in prison at Framingham Maximum Prison in Framingham, Massachusetts for life without parole.

Things escalated one Monday night, and the argument started because I was washing dishes, but I did not have on my wedding ring. He asked me about it, and I said that I did not need to wear it because it meant nothing to me. With that said, my husband grasped my hand and bent my ring finger back until it touched the back of my hand. I do not know if words were exchanged, but what I do know was that I was done! The next thing I knew was that the door in the kitchen leading to the parking lot of the complex was thrown open and my husband rushed out and sped away from the house in our Corolla, never to return. He called two weeks later asking if he could come and get his clothes, leaving me with no job and a three-year-old, and a mortgage to pay. My life was in turmoil, but I did not know that I was being *pierced for His purpose.*

This reminds me of a man who went to prison and was *pierced for His purpose.* His name was Joseph, and he was the 11th son of his father, Jacob. He was his father's favorite son, who was born to his beloved Rachael. Joseph started having dreams about his future and he would tell his brothers. The dreams angered his brothers. Joseph also told his father and his mother, and they too did not understand those dreams Joseph was telling them. I too, am a dreamer, and I would see things and they would come to pass.

God is into details so that you can get confirmation from Him that He is with you. God was with Joseph when he went from the pit to the prison and then from the prison to the palace. He was with me then, and I was going to learn how He would be with me for the rest of my life. He was my guide as a shepherd is to his flock.

The Lord is my shepherd; I shall not want. He maketh me lie down in green pastures: he leadeth me beside the still waters. He restoreth my soul: he leadeth me in the paths of righteousness for his name's sake. Yea, though I walk through the valley of the shadow of death, I will fear no evil: for thou art with me; thy rod and thy staff they comfort me" (Psalms 23 1-4 KJV). As a shepherd, God leads us through our life to the path of righteousness.

After my husband left, I started life with just my daughter and me. I had to go on welfare for one year because I was broke and all the bills in the house were, due. The only skill that I had was banking. So, when the welfare agency sent information about a class to learn computer accounting, I grabbed that opportunity. They sent me to Jewish Vocational Center, and they taught me computer skills. In the 90s, the computer was up and coming and I only knew how to type on a typewriter, but no other skills. After I graduated, I got a new job at Mellon Bank in Malden, Massachusetts. I started to attend services at my aunt's church which happened to be with the pastor who married my husband and me in 1985. The church moved around and finally settled in Dorchester, MA. I joined the church after I visited it one Sunday. I was only there a few months when Bishop Foxworth asked me to come to the front of the church, and he prophesied that I was called. I never heard that before. This was all new to me because my upbringing in the church where I was raised, did not give me this prophecy teaching. I did not know what being *called* meant, but I felt that it was right and was eager to know more about God in a new light.

After joining the church, they put me in the choir, and then a year later, I was put on the ministerial team as a young minister. I stayed in the choir because I loved the worship experience and ministering to the congregation. The choir was asked to visit Framingham Maximum Prison. As I was traveling to the prison, I heard a voice saying, "You are going in, but you are coming out".

I remained quiet, listening to this voice repeating this statement, over and over again. We had to go through many gates to get to the place where the prisoners were to convene for the service. We lined up on the opposite side of the room, and the prisoners came out in their orange jumpsuits. The minute I saw them, I started crying because I was wearing black and white, and they were wearing orange, and I saw my life across the room. I screamed and cried at the same time. It was like I was in a movie, watching them across the room and the words that I heard on the bus came back and were running through my head "You are going in, but you are coming out". I did not sing but cried the whole time.

A week after that encounter, I started studying *The Woman at the Well,* and I wrote a message called, "The Satisfied Woman". I did not know who I was going to preach that message to, but I knew that satisfied woman was me who got a drink from the well of salvation. A couple of days later I got a call from Rev. Clovis Turner, the chaplain of Framingham Maximum Prison, asking me to go with her to preach to the prisoners. I was shocked but ready to preach my message, "The Satisfied Woman". I went and preached to those women at Framingham Maximum Prison, and we were all in tears when the power of God came into the room. I told them that I too, was in prison-like them, and they came running to the altar when I asked them to come to receive Jesus Christ as their personal savior!

A year later, I was asked to join the ministerial team at Grace Church of All Nations in Dorchester, Massachusetts under the leadership of Bishop A. L. Foxworth where I have served there for 31 years. I was able to travel with the mission team to Manitoba, Canada to do world evangelism ministry with the World Evangelism Mission Team under the leadership of Evangelist Janet Langaigne. Later, I got to fulfill a dream and took a team of ministers to the Island of Barbados where I was born. We did a crusade for two weeks under my own ministry which is called Liberty International Ministries. This was a confirmation about how the spirit of the Lord spoke to me that I am called to the nations and would travel to specific countries. I have already completed crusades in two nations, in the same order that God spoke into my spirit in the 90s.

Presently, I am working on my ministry named Liberty International Ministries, to the nations, where I will be doing seminars, teaching, and working in the various churches where God sends me.

Notes On Overcoming:

_____

_____

_____

_____

_____

_____

_____

_____

_____

_____

Author Jillianne Veronica Harris

Author Jillianne Veronica Harris

Business owner and multimedia mogul, Jillianne Veronica Harris is not y our average woman. This insightful entrepreneur has achieved success and recognition in numerous endeavors and has become an exceptional inspiration to many.

Born as Veronica Jillianne Harris on November 30th, her mother believed she would grow to be a tenacious woman. After Jillianne's parents researched her name, (intellectual and honest, loyal, clever-minded, child of God, her parents changed her name to Jillianne Veronica Harris.

Jillianne is currently the CEO of her own company named *JaToj*. *JaToj* is a diverse entity that has both profit and non-profit divisions, and stands for JustATouchof_J. Through her company, Jillianne provides the world access to an array of innovative, nontraditional services. She continuously takes a bold and fearless approach in displaying her ever-evolving talents. Jillianne says that EVERYTHING she touches, she touches with God's guidance, so everything flourishes in its own capacity.

Jillianne is not only the Founder and CEO of her own corporation; this adventurous, intelligent, and well-educated entrepreneur is also a radio personality with her own podcast! However, her list of accomplishments continues. Jillianne owns her own fitness company called, *JustATouch of_JsFitness*. She is the creator of *MakingLoveinVsKitchen* cooking show, and one of Atlanta's very well-known personal chefs. Chef Veronica, or Chef V as she is known, is a Black Chefs Network partner who has established herself in the culinary arena as one of the best food and wine connoisseurs of her generation! Serving the east and west coast with her tasteful and embellished dishes, Jillianne's mission is to cultivate more love in each family she encounters through her food.

From Regional Healthcare Supervisor to mother, this Godly-profound woman is also an author and a future restaurant owner who has paved her way into the wine production industry, fitness apparel design, food distribution, her own radio show, TV series, and her own mobile app.

Jillianne is just trying to put it all out there in pieces for you, Baby! Everything else is God.

To connect with Author Jillianne Veronica Harris
and for all access to her entire JustATouchof_J Experience:
https://linktr.ee/mynameisroni76
Email - JustATouchof.j@gmail.com
Google her at #JustATouchof_J

Lost in the Sunshine

Where do I begin? This is *#JustATouchof_J*. I guess I gotta put it all out there in pieces for you, Baby! It's all about my life in the Sunshine. If you don't know what I'm talking about, let me explain. It's the shine of my life flowing through some of my darkest moments. See on November 1, 2020, I didn't know who I was. Was I Jillianne, Veronica, Jill, V, J, or Roniie because that's what they used to call me. By now I had only seen myself as *JustATouchof_J*. I had become that to so many. But who was I really? They say you're what you answer to. Now that I think about it in retrospect, I can say that I answered to God, or did I really?

As I walk down memory lane, I can remember praying every day, asking God to use me for His Glory. My desire was to inspire others for Him. So, let's start from the end, that's where it all began. That, my friends, is when I thought I started to win; but my life was backwards to the sunshine.

Y'all, I was so blind. I'm glad I can see my life differently now. For me, it's all about the little things. You know, the simple things in life that most of us take for granted. Things like food, water, and eyesight. The sight that enables many to see the green grass on a beautiful sunny day. Just picture the sun shining so bright like a diamond. That, I must say, is a blessing! I can remember the smell of fresh roses that I used to ignore. Those things, those things I'm now wishing I could endure. Those things, the little things like the taste of my amazing food. Those things are the things I took for granted! *Look at the birds of the air. They neither sow seed nor reap the harvest, but yet your Heavenly Father keeps feeding them. Oh, ye of little faith.* Matthew 6:26. This was the scripture I wrote on my bathroom mirror the day before it all happened. I didn't get the scripture then, but now, I know God was tempting me to go deeper. See, it was day 300 of my transforming through the renewing of my mind challenge. It had almost been nine months of me refocusing from past pain.

I can remember saying, "God please let them see you in me. Watching Bishop TD Jakes', "Believe" was my thing at that time. I can remember, I kept struggling with understanding that the predicament that I was in at that time, did not define my destiny. And let's not forget *him,* he was the love of my life. My Boo thing! The man of my dreams. The one I could've sworn God sent to me. Was it my downfall or my rise? So many lies tattooed within the truth. Our arms knew that history and for life, we will hold the rhythmic heartbeat of unity. Holding on to love had finally set us both free. Those are the little things. I can remember it was the intimacy around Labor Day 2020.

Now, I can also remember October. I gave my daughter Sa'Rai a surprise birthday party. I cooked everything she wanted. That was my last big meal. The look in her eyes melted my soul. It was like I had never seen her so happy as we snapped photos and recorded timeless videos. Her smile was so radiant!

I can now also remember my daughter Iman and I dancing and laughing during our photoshoot for my *JustATouchof_JsFitness* line, called JsFit. Lol, her laughter was mine. I can still see myself inside of her happiness. Her smile is something I will never forget. That day was absolutely amazing.

And my son, Taquam, I can remember the time we spent during the months before. It was nothing but complete spiritual healing. The hugs and tears diminished, so many years of the separation and not being thereafter he graduated from high school. But what was dope is that we all lived together again. It was just us four! Oh, and Baby! I can't forget him. I can remember him sitting by me every day; never leaving my side, like a dog that loved his owner. I'd rub my pit, and he'd rub his head on me, but it was like he knew something was wrong.

Those are the little things. Those are the memories I took for granted. The fact that I can remember them all now is a miraculous thing! Omg, today is August 17, 2021. Could you believe that seven months ago I couldn't remember anything? How can I go from running eight miles on the day that it all happened to now having no memory? I guess not being able to eat and drink anything, but water for two months straight can do that to you. I can remember January was the next month. January was the month I couldn't bathe myself, walk on my own, or see. It was the most frightening experience of my life.

I can remember the look on my children's faces. It was like they were saying, "Mommy, please don't leave me." I took so many things for granted! Was this my breaking point? That point where God could now use me for his glory because I finally wanted to live? Was I too late? By this point, I had lived inside a hotel, isolated for four months. All my funds were now gone. Y'all, I had nothing but God.

Then the unthinkable happened. A lab report revealed that I was suffering from severe mold toxicity. Five distinct types of molds were found inside my body. And to add insult to injury, my hair had fallen out, and my skin color had changed significantly because of my kidneys not functioning properly. My food consumption changed dramatically, too. Because my intestines separated, I was only able to eat six foods. And the Hyperosmia, which is defined as a "heightened and hyper-sensitive sense of smell" I developed was so bad! Can you imagine being able to smell something 50 feet away?

I couldn't even use soap to bathe because the smell was so strong. I had to wear three face masks just to complete the task. I can remember how I could smell through walls at this time! At one point,

I even thought I was losing my mind. No one could understand what I was going through, and I felt so alone.

But something deep down on the inside of me wanted to live. I kept saying, "God, please keep me." I cried every day because I just wanted to live. All I wanted to do was live and get better. I wanted others to see me overcome my ordeal. I wanted them to see my life in the sunshine. I can also remember when God told me to share my first testimony. How many of you know that He will speak to those who will listen? He said if I shared my testimony, I would be able to show so many people who He was. God said, "They need to see. He said they need to see you like this. With no hair and weighing only 100 pounds. They need to see the fear in your eyes, and the tears you cry."

Now, I also can now remember when my Godbrother, Turt came to see me. I hated to look at myself then because I was so thin. My temples were so sunk in on my face, that I turned every mirror around in my house. I even thought my daughters hated me because I was a wreck. I couldn't hold it together at all. My family was concerned; each day, my mother would stay on the phone with me for eight to ten hours at a time, just to help me through. Previously, these were things I couldn't remember.

The only thing I could hold on to every day was that I wanted to live. I fought and fought. Treatment after treatment. Appointment after appointment. Every time I tried to eat, I went into anaphylactic shock. I can remember my doctor even crying in front of me. She hated to see me so ill. I was like the woman in the Bible with the issue of blood. (Mark 5:24-34 and Luke 8:42-48). No one could help me! I went to doctor after doctor and all they would tell me was that there was nothing they could do to rectify my situation. Have any of you ever felt like everything you tried to do to help yourself didn't work? Well, that's how I felt! I felt so alone.

I remember walking outside my hotel one day. This was the day I questioned my life like Job in the Bible. I asked God, "Why am I here? Why do you allow me to suffer?" I remember that was the first day that I didn't want to live! It was like all the fight I had left was draining out of me.

Now, remember when I told y'all that the end was now in the beginning? The day I questioned my life, my 27-year-old son called. I broke down and told him that I couldn't do this anymore! "It's just too much! I cried." My son's exact words were, "Mom, come on, yes you can! What about your grandchildren?" I can admit I forgot about the *potential* of my future. None of my three children have children. If I gave up on myself, I wouldn't see my future grandchildren. Then my son said, "You started five businesses, Mom, and single-handedly managed them all. You raised us alone, Mom! You're an overcomer of so much! There was a pause before he continued.

"Mom, I lost my father at age three to suicide, he said. I didn't have my father, but I had you. Mom, you can do this! You can beat this! You're going to figure it out! Where's your faith in God? You always told us not to lose hope. You've got this, Mom! He went on and on with nothing but positivity; sharing words to motivate me.

So, I began to evaluate my thinking process! It was like God was showing me something. I realized that I forgot who I was. I had lost myself long before my health issue. I started to reflect on a lot of things after that conversation with my son. I asked God, "What are you trying to show me?" All he kept saying was, "Seek ye first the kingdom of God." So, I began reading my Bible more and listening to God's word any way I could get it. As I did this, God kept speaking to me more, and more. One day, He had my bestie, Maunieca, tell me that, "It's going to be big! He's going to use you for His glory!"

I suddenly remembered that was all I ever wanted in the first place! I mean, as far back as I can remember! When I was eight years old, I used to sing this song- *Lord, I'm available to you, my will I give to you, I'll do what you say to do. Use me, Lord. To show someone the way, enable me to say, my storage is empty, and I am available to you.* I can remember shaking my head and saying, "This is it! This is my testimony!"

God had to show me who I was, and most importantly, that when no one was with me, and I felt alone, He was there! Yes, I was like the woman with the issue of blood in the Bible. I started to believe that if I could just touch the hem of His garment, I knew I would be made whole again. God started to speak to me more and more through scripture, and he began to work on my character. He showed me so much about myself! He taught me about humility, my pride, and my insecurities. He showed me through seven months of trials and tribulations, that obedience is better than sacrifice! He reminded me of what He told Joshua in the Bible; *there should not any man be able to stand before thee all the days of thy life. As I was with Moses, so will I be with thee. I will not fail thee nor forsake thee!* Joshua 1: 5.

I started to see God's promises come true. I lived in a hotel for five months, with no job or any money, but every day, God provided my daily bread. He had so many people help me. He provided over $40,000 just so my living arrangements were adequate. He then provided so that I could get a new construction home built. In the process, God showed me who my real friends were, and those who were false from the beginning. I mean, there were so many magnificent accounts of Him bestowing His Glory!

I remember when God said to start recording my JustATouchof_J Podcast again. By this time, my life was going good and I was doing better. But God said, "I want you to be 100% honest and share your testimony."

He revealed that each of the challenges that I had passed had been a test, but others had been experiencing the same things. So, I started sharing my testimony. Because of that, I now have about 80k plays on multiple streaming networks. My Podcast is also played in over 150 different countries. One day I looked up and months turned into days. Before I knew it, I had gained 30 pounds. My hair had grown back. My skin had cleared, and I was jogging and working out again. My JustATouchofJ mobile app and podcast were popping like popcorn, Baby! And I put out another fitness apparel line at Thisisjustatouchof.j.com. I was even working on my online cooking show called, *Making Love in V's Kitchen* @MakingLoveInVsKitchen again! That's where I do my food thing. Plus, I was now the host of three different segments at a radio station, too. Do you see how everything shifted?

The greatest triumph was that I wasn't lost anymore! Y'all, I was blind, but now I can see. I now understand the name God had given to me in 2015, "JustATouchof_J". That was all that I needed! Everything else is God.

The moral of my story is, sometimes we literally forget who's we are. Although my enlightened experience emerged from my health trauma, I can be honest and say that it was good that I was afflicted. I had forgotten who I was long before this. My inner pain hurt, and insecurities had me doubting God's plan for my life. I wanted God to use me for His glory, but I let my inability to forgive myself and trust His guidance get in the way. In the end, I can now see the sunshine. I was **pierced for His purpose because** I'm **Destined to Win**! "This is JustATouchof_J, y'all! I just had to put that all out there in pieces for you baby."

Notes On Overcoming:

_____

_____

_____

_____

_____

_____

_____

_____

_____

_____

Author Kami Yvette Thomas

Author Kami Yvette Thomas

Kami Yvette Thomas was born in the seventies in Boston, Massachusetts into a close-knit family. Both of Kami's parents come from large families; her mother was one of twelve siblings and her father was one of fourteen. Kami has two siblings and is the mother of one child.

Professionally, Kami is a Cosmetologist. She loves to cook, dance, and travel. Kami hopes that her chapter will inspire others to heal past their brokenness so that they can live in prosperity, as God intended them to.

Connect with author Kami Yvette Thomas:
Instagram: @kamithomas123
Facebook: @KamiThomas

What You Become in Spite of What You Hear

Kami Yvette Thomas
A divine being, A gift from God, Twin.
That's what her name means biblically.
It was supposed to be Sharon Denise Thomas, but her
mom changed her mind at the last moment, Thank God!
Because every time she called her daughter-
Kami Yvette Thomas,
she was echoing into the atmosphere the meaning of her
name. *Kami Yvette Thomas* didn't know that at the time, nor
did she feel divine or like a gift.
See, what she knew about herself was that she was this coarse-
haired, long-faced, almond-shaped-eyed little girl, that was also
referred to as UGLY BLACKIE...
MONKEY, and if she somehow put them in an
antagonizing mood, they then would refer to her as
a PISSY-HEAD CREATURE FROM THE BLACK LAGOON.
Those venomous arrows launched her way,
hit her, and sent her down a path with detours-
several abortions and experiences of abuse;
see living out what she heard and dealing with life was hard,
but she is being forged by the best
BLACKSMITH there is... GOD!!!!

I thought the seventies was the best time to be born. A native of Boston, Massachusetts, from the city we call- *The Bury,* our sense of community was strong. People kept their eyes on what you were doing, and the kids played outside from early morning until the streetlights came on. Our families were closely knitted like a sweater; but like a knitted sweater, they sometimes had holes and that allowed uncomfortable temperatures and elements to creep in. Don't get me wrong, if you put the sweater on it seemed to do the trick for the moment, but unfortunately, with tumultuous Boston weather, you would need something that has more insulation. To prepare you for the ups and downs that life brings.

I was only six, in my elementary school years when your sense of self starts to develop. Learning how to read, understanding concepts and numbers, and decoding unfamiliar words, was supposed to be what I encountered. Instead, I learned how to accept the taunts that were hurled at me every day. UGLY: unpleasant and repulsive in appearance. That is what I was being told every time someone saw me and decided to replace my name with *that* word, and just dump how they felt on me. Emotional holes began to form which were deep like the pit of a pimple that had its due time to burst. With a poor sense of self-worth, engrafting onto me, leaving marks like a corkscrew plunged deep, twisting and squeezing like a boa constrictor. I began to see myself like what I HEARD!

When it was time to choose a path, I made a friend called *poor choices*; and she led me down the very road that mirrored the hurtful words projected onto me. Coming into my tween years, I was lifeless and changed rapidly because, in my head, I saw myself as unattractive, undesirable, and homely. You are probably saying, *"Why didn't you go tell your mom?"* I just didn't. I just accepted what no child should have and began to eat from the plate the world fixed for me. The truth be told, I didn't hear words of affirmation all the time from my mom, dad or brother. I lacked the ability to articulate how I was feeling and what I was going through. Yet, in those moments of verbal assaults, I wanted my mom to act like Medea. Lol, just be ignorant for a moment to get the job done! Then she could go back to her regularly scheduled program. *"But how could she have done what I needed her to do?"*, I thought to myself. For, if I had to describe her posture, it's a quiet confidence. She can say without saying or boasting and be without being loud or seen.

At fourteen, the character God intended me to have, was distorted. I had put on this gown of harmful, demeaning words and laid with them every night. I was like a vase that had been pushed off the counter and was fragmented into a billion pieces. At the age of fourteen, I lost my virginity and began sleeping around, and like Eve in the garden, eating the forbidden fruit, I became aware of the things God had no intentions of me finding out. I found out that low self-esteem and poor imagery of oneself make the worst friends ever. They will invite you over to hang out with them and fix you a place to sleep, making you think you have everything you need and that the bed they made for you is plush and warm. Then you find out they have you in the room on the floor, in the corner with just a throw, expose to everything coming and going. So, virginity had now packed her bags and here comes low self-esteem wrapped in this tall, chocolate package, shy-acting, sweet, strong, and seeming to love my family-oriented environment. He appeared very gentle; one who would never put me in harm's way. Boy, oh boy, the disillusionment of it all! I did not know then that I had just attracted the male version of myself. He needed to be affirmed that he was nice looking, smart and that he could do anything he set his mind to that his options were extensive.

Unfortunately, just like me, he too, made bad choices and started selling drugs and occasionally using them. He went from not being popular to slowly getting noticed and having the nicer things in life. Meanwhile, I was basing my worth on who I was with and how he gave this false sense of security and love; my bad was bad, but it got worse. Oblivious to the need of the six-year-old me and ignoring her original state of being, the gown that I wore then, had morphed into this backpack. The backpack was being filled like a lunch box that I kept eating out of. One day while snacking on some sadness, loneliness, and emptiness, I went for a walk just around the corner. To this day, I cannot remember which classmate it was that I ran into, but I will never forget it! He said, *"Hey, don't you go with such and such?"* I said, *"Yes."* And he goes, *"Well, he just went around the corner with what's her face.*" It was just like the atomic bomb dropped on Hiroshima. The already very little self-esteem I had was wiped out; he dumped me. Now you are probably saying everyone has their first heartbreak. That may be true, but mine was a dumping, a disposal of unwanted material, very careless and quick with no conversation, unlike a breakup where there is a discussion of your feelings, likes, or dislikes about each other, and the parties mutually agree to leave the relationship. I mean, hell, I didn't even get the opportunity to do my version of Tamar Braxton on him, putting to use my quick tongue, lol. This heartbreak moment didn't help the way I saw myself. So, I instantly said, "*WOW! I'M NOT PRETTIER than her?*" I mean she wasn't unattractive. it's just that she wasn't the total opposite of me, which then would have made more sense to me. So, because of that, I began to overcompensate in ACTING. I acted cute, pretty, tough, and sexy. I didn't feel like any of these words, nor did I fully understand the definition of them.

The seeds planted and that I helped water, grew this revolving door of disgust for who I was and what I was doing to my womb; the very thing God blessed me with to carry life. I found myself not only pregnant with life, but I was also pregnant with unworthiness. I remember being so scared the first time I got pregnant. I disconnected myself from what I was about to do.

I asked myself questions from the ending, *"Will I be able to go to school? Will I be able to go to the prom? Will I have to get a job?"* Very ignorant of where I was emotionally and mentally, unconscious and heedless behavior landed me right back at that same revolving door. See, the six-year-old was feeding the 14-year-old, regurgitated words that were implanted, infused, and reinforced from the world by me. Being an A+ long-time student of the School of Hard Knocks, I felt that it was time for a change. I needed to graduate from the revolving door of feeling ugly, homely, undesirable, and a whole lot of self-loathing moments. I had my cap and gown and was ready to walk down the aisle with all the pomp and circumstance.

I said to myself, *"Now, I'm ready to move forward and remove my cap and gown."* Then I quickly realized that my acting skills had me fooled. See, to think that I could start something or make a change in the midst of healing was absurd. I had to acknowledge the root; without acknowledging the root of my problem, my life turned into an epic fail! Now, out here in this ballroom of life, I found myself doing the tango with Mr. Abuse. This very structured dance of marked rhythms and abrupt pauses was something I was practicing all this time. See, I kept reinforcing this negative behavior that was unsolicited. I then taught myself how to prepare for Mr. Abuse; the venomous snake that would circle around me like a rattlesnake warning me with his rattle, and me not listening. I fell after the first strike, and the rattlesnake turned into a big ole anaconda, restricting me from being, from doing, and from healing.

Now those hurtful words were being expressed physically and every incident made me feel unworthy, not deserving respect, shameful, degraded, and dishonored.

Finally, I said to myself, "*I don't want to be the main actress in this movie any longer!*" I then enlisted myself into this war, this battle in my mind which I was determined to win. I had a little one that I was determined wasn't going to walk in my footsteps. So, I poured into him and said affirmations to feed his mind. I said affirmations like, "*There is nothing too hard, it's just new and unfamiliar. There's nothing wrong with being articulate, assertive, and well mannered.*"

Trying to teach something that I had very little knowledge of myself, and not having gotten watered enough myself, made it hard for me to water my son like he should have been watered. But God who is rich in mercy said, "*It starts with your inner self, and in order to get the full posture I have for you, you must know what I say about you. It starts in the mind and comes out of your mouth. Then you can start winning the battles and eventually winning the WAR! Mentally, when you speak out words, whether good or bad, they come from what you are exposed to.*" I thought about it and said, "*Right along with the bad, there was some good I was exposed to. There was good and bad growing together like the wheat and the tare.*" God said, "*If you ask me for wisdom and understanding in me, I will give it to you. I will allow your eyes to hear literally, what you see when you look in at yourself will not be what I whisper to you in your ear and in your heart. Right in the muck and the mire, I will give you*

112

stability and soundness in knowing who you are!!! Know that my words are life, not death, and they CAN NOT COME BACK VOID!"

So, I stepped out on faith, giving my broken, disappointed, ugly, unworthy, abused heart to Him, and accepted his word. I said, "God, take the fragmented vase that I am. I need You to seal me with your love so nothing harmful can get in." I gave him my gown and he began to wash it. I said, "Lord, here's my backpack that I was eating out of." He took it and He placed me at a table He had prepared right in front of my enemies.

Immediately, He said, *"Kami Yvette Thomas, am I not the one who spoke everything into existence, and put it in its proper place? Am I not the one who knows everything? Has the power to do anything and is perfectly good? Give me your brokenness, your hurt, your ugliness, your unworthiness, your poor choices, and abuse. And then watch your Sovereign God make you, the marred clay, into what I intended you to be!"* And He began to work the marred clay that was me, smoothing the imperfections out of me, pouring water on me so I wouldn't dry out, slamming me on the slab of forgiveness, applying pressure and pushing against me, knowing his intended outcome. He whispered in my ear, *"I am in the restoration business. I will return you to your former condition, I will revive you back to consciousness and deliver you from the powers of darkness, I will make your ears sensitive to my voice and I will make you more than a conqueror!"* So, I said, *"Sign me up! When can we start?"* The Lord said, *"We already started. I was just waiting on you to simply HEAR MY VOICE!"*

Notes On Overcoming:

Notes On Overcoming:

_____

_____

_____

_____

_____

_____

_____

_____

_____

_____

Author Lisa Thomas-El

Author Lisa Thomas-El

Lisa Thomas-El, is a passionate woman, who is also called the Goddess of Love. She is a native of Camden, New Jersey. She is the mother of three adult sons and one adult daughter. She is proud to be the grandmother of numerous grandchildren through her adult sons and those that have adopted her as their grandmother.

Her journey of life led her to choose a career as a Substance Abuse Counselor, with a license as a Clinical Alcohol and Drug Counselor (LCADC). She served in this capacity for 16 years after securing her master's in Human Services from Lincoln University. She has always had a great passion for people and assisting them in connecting with the whole parts of themselves. This has led her to establish a Facebook community called, *Being Authentically Me* and being a part of a *21-Day Self-Love Journey*. The intentions of these groups are to extend a message of love and healing to those seeking greater connections.

During the last four years, Lisa has also worked as an In-home therapist serving families and their youth. This has fulfilled her passion to be compassionate and to serve the needs of others. Lisa is also a co-author in the compilation series, *Destined to Win: Volume 3*, and *Inner Monologue*. In addition, she is a podcaster on *Lite* Creationz. Spotify

To connect with the Author Lisa Thomas El:
Facebook: @LisaThomasEl
Facebook Group: @BeingAuthenticallyMe
Email: lisathomasel@gmail.com

I See You!

I see you! I see the uncertainty in your eyes, seeking to be seen with love and acknowledgment. I see you yearning to be held in the arms of love for safety and comfort. I see you with your innocence, beauty, and grand spirit. Yet, you stand in this space of life with questions and the need for reassurance.

I see you! I see the infant that smiles and gurgles at the sight of others who smile back at her. I see the exuberance of love that radiates from you, looking for the modeled reflection to shine back at you. I see you as you're wobbling to take your steps and constantly failing until you have gained certainty in your ability to stand and move forward. You've got it! Here you stand, walking effortlessly and traveling about with great ease.

I see you throughout your stages of development. I see the young lady that feels a sense of awkwardness in her body and mind. I see you wanting and trying to belong in a space where you have never felt that you belonged. I see you as you're seeking to belong. To belong in the spaces for which you've traveled. In these travels, you were in the presence of your mother, grandparents, and father.

Who are you in these spaces? Who are you expected to be? For whom are these expectations derived?

I see the confusion that lies within. The confusion of who you are, who you are to be, and who shall you become. These questions have led you through a broad range of experiences. These experiences have been the cornerstone of your existence. During the various times and life situations that you've lived, you have been on a journey to seek a deeper meaning for your existence. Yet it has been through these experiences that you have come to connect with your soul's purpose.

As I reflect back to the developmental stage of my 5-year-old self, I feel her shame and uncertainty of who she is. She attempts to fit in with those around her with her giddiness. However, it is not reciprocated. It is looked upon as an utter annoyance by the adults who she seeks to please. The feeling of shame electrifies her body and reminds her that her behavior is not well received. I see the elongation of her face each time she attempts to connect with others, and it is not received. Yes, I see you as you attempt to sleep each night in the darkness awaiting the morning to come and bring the presence of your grandmother, who returns after working the overnight shift. However, within those nights lurked confusion. Confusion lay within my bed as a disguise for security. Holding and caressing the little fragile body as she is fondled and stroked. Words of comfort, spoken into her ears despite the confusion that trembled within her body. This doesn't feel right! You are supposed to be my protector! My protector from those who would seek to physically harm me. Yet here you lie within my sheets?

How do they not see? How do they not see what's taken place? How does the presence of stained blood on these sheets not serve as an indicator that a violation has taken place? How do they ignore what seems to be so obvious and in plain sight? Yes, I see you! I see the hurt and pain that lurks within. I see the smile slowly fading into a frown. I see you seeking to find a connection within this disconnection.

The years pass by, and the disconnection seems to widen. The depth and width of the disconnection or impacted by the people in my life and by my spirituality. Do they even exist? What does this all mean? I seek began to seek answers to these questions that were within me, from outside sources. I was seeking an understanding of the meaning of life. As the stages of my development continued forward, the questions seemed to get bigger. Is it in another that my connection is found?

Stepping out of self and reflecting back, I see you as you seek acceptance from others. This began within your family. The ones closest to you, yet feelings of alienation surrounded you. You ask, "Who am I to be?" I see you surrounded by others while feeling invisible throughout it all. Being the observer of adults that appeared to be "having fun," while you, this young child, struggled to breathe. You tend to suffer in silence; never offering others a clue to your demise. Do they not see your struggles? Or has the invisibility of your essence been confirmed throughout this experience as another reminder of your insignificance?

Now, you are a young woman; you are still yearning for love and acceptance. I see you seeking to be seen in a world that does not acknowledge you as an instrumental part of life. Yet, I see you. I see this young woman wanting to eliminate her existence as a means of being seen. How does she gain acknowledgment within this invisible cloak? I see you looking to be seen. Strutting yourself down the street, looking to be acknowledged as a beautiful young Queen. Yet, all you see in the mirror is an empty shell surrounded by skin. Your physique is shapely, yet you are shamed for each curve that graces your body. As you are being acknowledged, you are trapped by the sweet sounds and affirming words that have led you into a shed that is dark and cold. Within these walls are three males that have spoken the words your ears have longed to hear. Yet the actions which they bestowed upon you only caused you more suffering. Again, you retreated into silence.

I see you, and I remember. My inner voices reminded me that I only needed to "act normal", as if nothing out of the ordinary was taking place. Despite the pain my body endured, my mind kept me focused and in control. As I "acted normal", I walked away as if it was just another day.

I walked away with the inner voices warning me, "There's no way you can tell your parents because you're going to get in trouble for walking down *that* street". This subtle reminder sealed the agreement - "I would not tell". So, this secret remained within, as my invisibility cloak began to flourish.

I see you! I see the shame, guilt, remorse, and pain that you carry within. I see you wanting and yearning to be loved. I see you making poor choices about your relationships. I see the eye that has been blackened and the bruises on your skin that remind you that "love hurts". It hurts because you have been reminded of the need for this infliction to take place to assure your obedience.

"Well, don't they see?! Doesn't anybody see ME!!!! Doesn't anybody see the suffering that has been going on for way too long? Do they not see it in my isolation? Do they not see it in my behavior, that I desperately seek love and acceptance from others? Do they not see it in my tears at night, as I tremble in fear of what may be lurking in the night as I attempt to rest?"

Yet, I see you. I see you wanting to be free. I see you wanting to free yourself from the chains that keep you bound and abandoned. I see the pain that streams through your veins wanting to be released as a reminder of your existence. "Do I matter? Do you matter? Do we matter? These are the questions that have plagued me throughout my life. It has been through these darkest moments that I have sought some sort of relief. It has been in these moments of desperation that I sought the elimination of *Self*. The *Self* that carried her pain as a badge of honor. The *Self* that wanted to be rescued. The parts of me that felt that I would only be valued through sorrow. The part of me that spoke of my pain only to seek to be rescued.

I see you as you seek to be rescued. Rescued by men in exchange for sex to validate your mere existence. I see you as you seek to be validated through the choices you made with your consumption of alcohol and drugs. Seeking acceptance from others while engaging in poisons that darkened your path while igniting your suffering. I see the road you've traveled was an attempt to belong; yet left you feeling even more secluded in your darkness. The road you traveled led you to the depths of despair. I see you seeking to eliminate the parts of you that remain in the dark.

I see you! I see the numerous attempts you've made to eliminate the *Self* that existed. I saw you consume bottles of pills and I saw the self-inflicted slashes to your body to release the pain that remained inside. I see you! Yet it has been in your darkest moments that you have sought the light. The darkness is where your deepest questions seek to be answered. It has been the *Self* that you have encountered that demonstrated who you're not in order for you to reconnect with the truth of who you are.

Did you not see that your darkness was the light? The darkness served its purpose, as you serve others. These spaces were never permanent dwellings for you to reside, just a temporary placement. Your journey has been **pierced for a purpose**. It has been in the moments of darkness that you've surrendered to your faith. Faith that was not focused on what you could see, but faith that surpassed understanding.

It was in the darkest moment when I took back my life and sought for greater understandings of my experiences. It was in the moment of surrender that I was willing to see the darkness as light. The moment when I cried out, asking for the way through. The moment when I no longer sought someone to blame but asked what it was that I was to learn from these experiences. That was the moment when my life shifted.

I see you, seeking truth. I see you seeking connections. Not just the connections that bound you with another, but the connections that allow your soul to soar.

It was in the moment of surrender that I looked at my life's story to see the gifts it was presenting me. I see the little girl that once lived her life as if her innocence no longer existed. This is a fallacy created within her mind. I see her child-like innocence has always remained within her. Her desire to continue to seek and open her heart and mind to grander possibilities was and is a reflection of her child-like curiosity.

As I reflected, I found myself. I saw that I grew weary from my experiences of seeking my worth through others and things. Yet it has been in these exact moments that I was *pierced for a purpose* beyond imagination! The shell I wanted to die was the part of me that was transitioning to another stage of living. The moment I surrendered; I became aware. My awareness was based on love. I let go of the expectations I had of others to make me whole. I let go of the need to blame others and hold them accountable for their wrongdoing. Instead, I allowed love to shower me with worthiness and forgiveness.

So often we tend to believe that forgiveness is letting others off the hook for their transgressions when it's really serving as the key to unlocking the chains that have entangled you in despair and defeat. My experiences have been the road map to my purpose. It's far too easy to walk in faith when all of life is golden and the road is smoothly paved. Yet, it's in the moments of transgression that we can reach out, open up, and allow the grandest version of ourselves to unfold.

Even as I write this chapter and speak to others, I recognize that this has only been one aspect of who I've been. Yet in this moment, I feel free! I'm no longer chained to the story of my past that has constantly reminded me of who I've been, and the necessity to create worth despite who I've been. You see, the story of your past is just the journey through your life. It can be validation that you are an overcomer!

The gift of my life is that it has allowed me to grow wiser and have a yearning for living. As I explore the gifts which I have been given, I can rejoice. I rejoice that the gift of healing has been circulated within and throughout my life and the lives of others. My stories have provided me the ability to have compassion, empathy, and understanding of another's struggles and to support them through them.

The writing of this chapter has been a great gift! It has allowed me to reflect on the numerous times when I didn't see clearly and thought that there was simply no way beyond the hollow space, I was in. But here I AM, writing out a part of my life's story to serve as a message of hope, love, and forgiveness. I say forgiveness, to myself and others, because I see that there was never anyone holding me back from the gifts that are within me. God has always been my light of love throughout my journey and that means that none of the stumbling steps I took were to punish me. On the contrary, God held me up in the highest regard of love

I can see clearly now that each aspect of me is a combination of the restored part of ME. The Me that stands in faith, triumph, and reassurance that the Love of God has always prevailed. I stand in and with this truth as I've been *pierced for a purpose.* I stand tall, firmly believing that my Journey Continues!

Notes On Overcoming:

_____

_____

_____

_____

_____

_____

_____

_____

_____

_____

Notes On Overcoming:

_____

_____

_____

_____

_____

_____

_____

_____

_____

Author Lisa Martin

Author Lisa Martin

Lisa Martin is a native of Boston, Massachusetts. She is the author of the self-published booklet, *Consecrated One*, which was released in 2010. Lisa is an honor graduate of Marblehead High School and received the John Hancock Honors Award. In 1988 she earned a Bachelor of Science Degree in Business Administration and Management from Fitchburg State College and was on the Dean's List. In 1992 Lisa received a Diploma in Basic Biblical Studies from C.H. Mason Bible College in Boston, Massachusetts under the Tutelage of her Pastor, Dr. David Ancrum.

In 2004 Lisa became an Ordained Pastor under Apostle Helen Watkins-Skeete of Love Unlimited Ministries in Boston, Massachusetts. Lisa loves the Lord with all her heart and is sold out to him. Lisa especially has a passion for Intercessory Prayer and Women's Ministries. She is the Founder of *Prayer is my Passion Ministries* and has been hosting Intercessory Prayer since 2003. Lisa also established *God's Woman of Excellence Ministries* and has hosted Women's Bible Studies and Women's Intercessory Prayer in 2004 and 2008 respectively.

In 2011, Lisa established *Virtuous Lady's Enterprises* where she makes custom lap scarves, handkerchiefs, women preachers' towels, warfare prayer pillows and so much
More.

In her spare time, Lisa enjoys several hobbies: reading, journaling, and inspirational writing, sewing, listening to old-time radio podcasts, word search puzzles, water aerobics, and collecting dolls and toys.

To connect with the author:
Facebook & Instagram: Pastor Lisa Martin
Business Facebook: Virtuous Lady's Enterprises
YouTube Channel: A Passion for God
Ministry Facebook: Prayer is my Passion Ministries
Emails: lisaamartin0808@gmail.com
virtuousladysenterprises@gmail.com

Paralyzed by Grief

"They are blessed who grieve, for God will comfort them"
Matthew 5:4 NCV

New Year's Day has always been my favorite holiday. It is the time of the year where we have great expectations, new goals, and celebrations. For me, it starts on New Year's Eve when I normally attend Watch Night Service at church. This is a service when we praise the Lord in song and share testimonies of our experiences of the past year. Then we all look forward to hearing the Word of God from the Preacher that usually has a theme to empower us and carry us through the New Year Season. When midnight strikes, we would all give a loud shout of thanksgiving unto the Lord; grateful that we made it and crossed over to the New Year.

I remember from back in the day when we would have concerts and midnight musicals after our Watch Night Services. Oh, what a time we would have praising the Lord and dancing in the Spirit. Various soloists and choirs would sing songs of praise and worship unto the Lord. I also recall New Year Revivals for the first week of the year that extended for a few days, weeks, and sometimes for the entire month of January. These services were very inspirational and empowering. Our souls were revived! We were ready to conquer anything that opposed us. I was grateful to be a part of these days!

However, on January 1, 2016, it was a New Year's Day like no other. This was the day that I lost my Beloved Mother, Barbara Estelle Martin. My life has changed forever since that day. Her passing shook me to my core, and I took it very hard. We were extremely close. You could say that I was her hip baby. We had a great relationship. She was the Matriarch of our family, and she has been sorely missed. My mother raised my sister Cynthia, and me in a very loving, yet strict, Christian household. We were brought up in a Pentecostal Church that we attended faithfully. We were in church every Sunday beginning with Sunday School and then Morning Worship. We then returned to church on Sunday evenings, Wednesday nights for Prayer and Bible Study, and then Friday nights for Evangelistic Service. We were also very active members of auxiliaries. My mother was an usher and the Treasurer of the Sunday School department. My sister and I were members of the Young Adult Choir and the Youth Ministry. At the time, I did not like being in church all the time. However, as an adult, I am very appreciative of the foundation that I received being raised in the fear and admonition of the Lord.

In November of 2014, my mother was diagnosed with early-stage Vascular Dementia as a result of Congestive Heart Failure. Dementia is a loss of brain function that occurs with certain diseases. It affects memory, cognition, language, judgment, and behavior. As a result, she was no longer able to live independently, and I became her Primary Fulltime Caregiver. I took care of her for the last thirteen months of her life. This was very challenging for me as I had never cared for anyone before. I did not experience motherhood, so this was very new to me. I assisted my mother with bathing and dressing, cooking her meals, doing her laundry, and house cleaning. I was exhausted all the time. I would sit with her and watch our favorite TV shows, including Christian TV. I helped her water her plants. She had such a green thumb. Unfortunately, her type of dementia is very aggressive, and it accelerated very quickly. She began to sleep a lot. Her cognitive skills declined, and she was unable to hold a conversation, she was losing mobility and became confined to a wheelchair and ultimately became bedridden. We sought Hospice Care which she had at home for the last six months of her life.

On New Year's Eve, December 31, 2015, my mother's breathing was very labored, and I knew she did not have long. All my family gathered together, this day, as she went into a deep sleep. My Spiritual Mother, Apostle Helen Watkins-Skeete, came to our house and stayed with my sister, Cynthia, and me as we sat at my mother's bedside. We sang hymns, praised and worshiped the Lord, and we prayed for Mother as she transitioned from this earth. I watched my mother take her last breath between 3:30 pm and 3:40 pm on Friday, January 1, 2016. I could not believe she was gone. She taught me everything I know except how to live without her.

Thus begins my journey of Grief. Grief is a very difficult, but necessary process. Everyone experiences it differently. I experienced severe grief. Losing my Beloved Mother was extremely painful, and it left a huge void in my life. She was my Best Friend and my Personal Intercessor. She was supportive to me personally and in my ministry. She loved me unconditionally. There is nothing like a Mother's Love to nurture you, as well as to correct you. How am I going to live life without her?

I began to weep uncontrollably daily, all day long. I could barely think straight. I was so distraught and consumed with grief. I thought about her constantly and began to weep more because I could never hear her voice again or her contagious laugh. I could not embrace her ever again with a hug. My mother was gone. I could not celebrate her birthday or mine with her again. I could not enjoy the things that we loved to do together such as watching our favorite crime drama TV shows. I could not have breakfast with her homemade waffles or her homemade yeast bread rolls with butter and Karo Dark Corn Syrup or share a Domino's pizza or a PuPu Platter from our favorite Chinese restaurant.

I also experienced severe depression. I missed my mother. I wanted my mother. "Why did you take my mother from me, Lord?" I prayed for her healing from dementia, for which there is no cure. I prayed for her body to be restored. I knew that there was nothing too hard for God. He is a God of Miracles. "In my Prayer Ministry, I have agreed in prayer for others that needed a miracle and answer to prayer, and you came through for many of them. Why didn't you answer this one personal prayer of mine to heal my mother?"

I then began to experience Anger. I was angry that I lost my beloved Mother. I was angry that my life has changed forever. I began to take my frustration out on my loved ones. I was a ticking time bomb, consumed with grief and very fragile emotionally. I did not like the person I had become. This was not me. I was not myself. What was wrong with me? I could not sleep at night and suffered severe insomnia. I lost my desire to read the Bible. I also lost my desire to pray. How could I pray to a God that I was mad at? This was so out of character for me. This was not Lisa. Who have I become? I was so miserable. I was tormented with grief. Webster's New Collegiate Dictionary defines the word- torment as *extreme pain or anguish of body or mind, agony.* I did not want to live anymore. I certainly did not enjoy living life without my mother. I asked the Lord to take me from this earth because this grief I was experiencing was unbearable. I cried out, "No one understands how I am feeling!" The phone calls, texts, and cards had stopped coming months ago and now it was several years since my mother had transitioned. "How come I can't move forward with my life? I want to but I can't for some reason. I know my Beloved Mother would not want me to live like this. She would want me to live my Best Life."

Finally, I have had enough! I refuse to live like this. I will no longer live a defeated life. I will not let grief torment me another day. I cried out to the Lord and repented for neglecting my salvation so greatly. I apologized for my anger in His decision to take my mother. God is Sovereign! I now realize that I was Paralyzed by Grief. Webster's New Collegiate Dictionary defines the word- Paralysis as "loss of the ability to move, a state of powerlessness or incapacity to act." I began to take Authority Spiritually and Declare that I will no longer be paralyzed by grief in Jesus' name. I realized that my Healing and Deliverance required my Participation! I am thankful for my loved ones and friends that had been interceding for me. However, I had to make a conscious effort to renew my mind through the Word of God; to Restore my relationship with the Lord by spending Quality Time with him in Prayer and Devotion. This is my Journey of Grief and my Process for Healing. It did not happen overnight. It took me five years to get to the place that I am at today. A place of Freedom and Victory.

I recall a scripture that comforted me from the Book of Lamentations: *It is of the Lord's mercies that we are not consumed because his compassions fail not. They are new every morning; great is thy faithfulness. The Lord is my portion, saith my soul; therefore, will I hope in him. The Lord is good unto them that wait for him, to the soul that seeketh him.* (Lamentations 3:22-25 KJV)

You may be at the place where I was when I was suffering from severe grief. You want to move forward but you are Paralyzed. You don't have to live like this any longer. You can get through this. You can be Whole again. I am a Living Witness, and this is my Testimony. Will you allow the Lord to Heal you from this excruciating pain of grief? It will require your Participation! I encourage you to reach out for help from your loved ones, a spiritual leader, such as a pastor or mentor and if need be, seek professional help. There are therapists that are trained and even specialize in grief counseling.

Quotation:

Grief is not a disorder, a disease, or a sign of weakness. It is an emotional, physical, and spiritual necessity, the price you pay for love. The only cure for grief is to grieve. ~Dr. Earl A. Grollman, Author of *Living when a Loved One has Died*

Notes On Overcoming:

Author Melinda Tharps Daughtry

Author Melinda Tharps Daughtry

Melinda Tharps Daughtry was the only child of the late Barbara Lynn Hall. Melinda is a native of Boston, Massachusetts. As a single teenage mother, she raised two sons while residing in Mission Hill Public Housing.

Graduating with honors from Bunker Hill Community College, Melinda received an associate degree in science. She works as a radiology technologist at Boston Medical Center, a nonprofit hospital in the city of Boston. There she performs routine screening and diagnostic mammograms on a diverse group of people, providing outstanding care without exception.

On September 22, 2018, she became a ram in the bush. She married an extremely impressive man of God, William Daughtry whom she prayed for, claimed, and prophesied. Melinda now resides in Randolph, MA with her awe-inspiring hubby and her loving cockapoo puppy "Poppy".

Melinda is a wife and a friend to her superb husband. She is also a supporter and motivator to a delightful son and the faithful, loyal friend and encourager to many. Melinda always wants to see the good in every person and situation. Most importantly, she takes great interest and pleasure in interceding on behalf of God's people through the Power of Prayer.

To connect with the author:
Facebook: @melinda.tharps
Email: melindatharps@gmail.com

My Faith is All I Need

I am a plant, radiant, emanating great love, joy, and happiness. Blooming, flourishing, thriving in vigor, blushing, bold with a well-developed root system. I have a vital role in keeping people, animals, and the earth healthy. My elements provide food, medicine, shelter, but most importantly produce oxygen. It's vital that I thrive so that humans can survive. I am essential for life! Once a healthy, vibrant, well-developed plant that bloomed. Then life happened! An unexpected tragedy. What was once a healthy plant that grew, started deteriorating. Dried up; it was shrinking, declining, decaying, fading, wasting. A plant that had lost freshness, pale and unwell, experiencing a lack of nutrients. Disease resulting from a loss affected parts lost their turgidity and drooped. Drooping leaves when it is moved and feeling stressed. Roots that were once mature and advanced, have been adversely affected, developing root rot.

In all honesty, I truly do not know where to begin. First and foremost, I give honor where honor is due. I glorify my Lord and Savior for keeping me, covering me, protecting me, as well as carrying me while allowing me to go through the process. My pastor, Melanie Turner-Kirkland once said, "from the process always proceed the promise." Therefore, I was *Pierced for a Purpose*.

At the age of sixteen, I gave birth to my second child. Even though it may have seemed aberrant to become a teen mom at such an early age, God knew and predicted my life while I was in the womb of my beloved mother. The seed of the womb is a blessing from the Lord. The morning of June 16, 1989, I delivered a healthy baby boy weighing 6 pounds 16 ounces, Richard Tia Terrance King, Jr. Fearfully and wonderfully made in the image that the father intended. How precious were my thoughts of him; he was handsomely featured, and pleasantly dispositioned, refined, a bundle of joy! I must say it was tough being a single mother raising two sons. Like any other mother, all I ever wanted was the best for my boys, from infancy to adulthood, and beyond. I molded and shaped my son's life by leading by example. While I didn't graduate from high school, I did receive my GED. I then attended Bunker Hill Community College and graduated with certification as a medical assistant. When my boys were about the ages of five and six, I landed a job at Brigham and Women's Hospital, where I worked as a medical assistant on the labor and delivery floor, while living in Mission Hill Public Housing. Raising my young boys, I knew that the characteristics that I displayed would shape their future for growth, reproduction, and functional activities. It was exceptionally hard as a teenage mother raising boys to become men. Simultaneously, each of my boys was coming into themselves. I would constantly pray over them! Asking God to shield them with His divine covering of defensive protection from any and everything that may come at them or against them. I pleaded the blood covering upon them.

All you hear in our inner cities is news about a person taking another person's life. You can never turn on the TV without hearing about or seeing a fatality.

I would say to myself, "Lord, I don't know what I would do if I lost one of my sons. I would lose my natural mind."

I couldn't begin to imagine that ever happening to me. Notions would ponder in my mind, "How could God allow someone to go through something so extreme?" In this world we reside in, there is a spirit of hate, deceit, jealousy, malice, racism, and murder.

Perhaps the most bitter experience in my life was on July 31, 2011. My son, Richard Tia Terrance King, Jr. was murdered on the streets of Boston. The seed of my womb that was a blessing from the Lord, was gone! Life happened to me! I was numb, devastated, heartbroken, and extremely depressed. My heart was gone and my soul-wounded. I felt pain in a way that I never felt before. The very thing I prayed about continuously without ceasing, asking God for protection over my sons to keep them safe from hurt, harm, and danger, seen and unseen, had happened! The very images seen on the news, I was now experiencing. I couldn't wrap my head around it. Why would God allow tragedy to come to my home when I was on my knees seeking and crying out to Him? There were so many unanswered questions that I needed answered. "Why God, why are you allowing me to suffer?"

God gives life, His character goes into the creation of every person. So how could another human being have the audacity to take what the creator created? I was broken and stuck. Possibly still have that broken and stuck mentality, concealed, allowing it to lay dormant. I'm hurting over the loss of my child. This traumatic drama has affected my emotional well-being. I go through the normal daily functions, yet I function while being dysfunctional. Internally weeping, having a yearning desire for justice!

Eventually, I felt a nudge; entrusting God I'm assured and deeply at peace. In this godless world, you will undergo difficulties. However, no matter how harsh our trials, or how seemingly hopeless our situation, look for God's caring touch. He provides in ways that go beyond our narrow definitions or expectations. Yet, going through this deeply distressing trauma shut me down! Satan tried to attack my mind and drive a wedge between God and me. Nevertheless, knowing what I know, only God could bring me through this extreme physical and mental suffering I was enduring. I brought tranquility to my tormented mind and hollow heart by focusing on the word of God. One of my favorite passages of scriptures is Philippians 4:6-9 (AMP): *Do not be anxious or worried about anything, but in everything (every circumstance and situation) by prayer and petition with thanksgiving, continue to make your (specific) requests known to God. And the peace of God (that peace which reassures the heart, that peace) which transcends all understanding, (That peace which) stands guard over your hearts and your minds in Christ Jesus (is your). Finally, believers, whatever is true, whatever is honorable and worthy of respect, whatever is right and confirmed by God's word, whatever is pure and wholesome, whatever is lovely and brings peace, whatever is admirable and of good repute; if there is any excellence, if there is anything worthy of praise, think continually on these things (center your mind on them, and implant them in your heart). The things which you have learned and received and heard and seen in me, practice these things (in daily life), and God (who is the source) of peace and well-being will be with you.*

I was compelled to have quietude in my mind, so I made a conscious decision to forgive. The word says in Colossians 3:13 (NIV)- *Bear with each other and forgive one another if any of you had a grievance against someone. Forgive as the Lord forgave you.*

It has become my heart's desire to pray and intercede on behalf of the individuals that are responsible for my son's murder. God graciously offers forgiveness of sins. I am a product of God's image, as a result, I in return, graciously offer forgiveness to the perpetrators. I know what I do. How I behave during the process is a direct result of my spiritual condition. I couldn't let the immorality in my heart hinder my relationship with God. For that reason, I prayed regarding those who murdered my son. Asking the Father to remove the blinders from their eyes, for they know not what they do. The bible says-

The heart is deceitful above all things and is extremely sick; who can understand it? I the Lord search the heart and test the mind, to give every man according to his ways, according to the fruits of his deeds. (Jeremiah 17: 9-10 ESV).

I have made an emotional, earnest appeal to God for their protection knowing that they sold themselves to do evil in the eyes of the Lord. I wanted no hurt, harm, or danger to come upon them. I couldn't visualize another mother grieving and burying a child at the age of twenty-two. I prayed that they are marked like Cain who killed his brother Abel in the Book of Genesis. Warning anyone who might come for them. I wanted no part of revenge in any shape, form, or fashion. I binded that murderous spirit and loosed it with unity, peace, and love amongst our youths, in this world. But above all, I prayed that they would have an encounter with the Creator, as Saul had on the road to Damascus. *"Father, consume them and breathe life into them as they confess to the truth, repent, and ask for forgiveness while surrendering unto you."*

God is all-seeing, all-knowing, all-powerful, and ever-present. Someone has information or witnessed the demise of my son. God knows who you are. A word of knowledge: you're not sinless because you didn't commit the act. You have allowed Satan to hinder and attack you with lies and deception. You aided Him in his work by covering up the wrong that was done. Ask God to deliver you from the guilt of bloodshed. No sin is too great to be forgiven. He can and will forgive any transgression. "Father, deter them from within, clear their hearts and spirits for new thoughts and desires to do what is just. Right conduct can come only from a clean heart and spirit. Although you have blood on your hands you can still be redeemed by the blood of the Lamb. Receive His forgiveness, so that you can move from alienation to intimacy, from guilt to love. My Pastor once preached the message- *You can't heal what you conceal.*

It has been ten years since the death of my son. The case is considered a cold case. God continues to tenderly heal my deep loss. Through the Holy Spirit, God promised me, years prior that, "Justice will prevail." The Holy Spirit reminded me of my son's words of encouragement. He was my number one ego booster on numerous occasions. He would say, "Mom, I'm so proud of you! You work two jobs while going to school: you're my inspiration!"

At the time of my loss, I was a full-time employee at Harvard Vanguard Medical Associates, working part-time at St. Elizabeth Hospital, while attending college to become a Radiology Technologist at Bunker Hill Community College. My faith in my Savior, as well as holding on to my beloved son's words of affirmation allowed me to press towards the mark for the prize of the high calling. I graduated with honors, with an associate degree in science despite my professor's suggesting that I take leave to heal. People expected my faith to die; from a human's perspective, doubt is understandable.

It was Thursday, June 17, 2021, which is the day after my son's birthday. I was speaking in my heavenly language during my prayer time while driving into Boston. During my prayer, the Holy Spirit spoke to me saying, "I made a promise to you ten years ago, I'm not a man that I should lie. If I said a thing, I shall perform it. Are you of little faith? Wait! Be still and know that I AM who I AM".

God answers prayer in His own way and His own time. He works in impossible situations. I'm self-assured that God will allow justice to prevail.

Prayer reaffirms my aspiration. Yes, ten years may appear as evidence that justice for my family and me shall not triumph, yet I will not compromise my faith. I will maintain my integrity with a determined mindset. Therefore, I live by faith and not by sight. This situation may appear dead, but the resurrection power that resides within me will resurrect this very thing that seems dead. *The hand of the Lord was on me, and he brought me out by the Spirit of the Lord and set me in the middle of a valley; it was full of bones. He led me back and forth among them, and I saw a great many bones on the floor of the valley, bones that were very dry. He asked me, "Son of man, can these bones live?" I said, "Sovereign Lord, you alone know." Then he said to me, "Prophesy to these bones and say to them, Dry bones, hear the word of the Lord!* (Ezekiel 37; 1-4. NIV)

The Lord does not keep us from encountering life's storms, He sees us through them. I will never give up my hope and expectations, the Holy Spirit can only move through the degree of my faith. I can recall my pastor saying, "faith activates the promises." There is a spoken promise over my life. I refuse to let the nay-sayers deactivate my faith or the promise. An investment into my faith will not only produce the promise but will add to my testimony.

June 25, 2021, at 11:24 A.M. I am reflecting on my past. Having a heart of gratitude for my presence. Meanwhile, humbly waiting with great anticipation for God's plans. Lifting my eyes unto the hills, while indulging in enjoyable recollection of my child's spoken words. Through God's Holy Spirit, my faith quiets my heart and I trust God's promise while staying encouraged. These are my source of nourishment.

The Lord is my Shepherd, I lack nothing. I'm completely dependent on my Shepherd for provision, guidance, and justice. In trusting in Him, I have immeasurable peace. I'm not fazed or intimidated by the lack of the years that have passed. I'm in a state of contentment because my Shepard Father has offered me internal comfort. Minister Sandy Clermy, once said, "Staying in position produces a promise of VICTORY in your purpose."

In the end, God is in control, fighting this battle for me. He and only He knows how to triumph.

Travis Greene once sang, "*I'm going to see the victory, I'm going to see the victory, for this battle belongs to you, Lord.*" Jesus gave me an extraordinary message. (John 12:24 NLT). *I tell you the truth unless a kernel of wheat is planted in the soil and dies, it remains alone. But its death will produce many new kernels, a plentiful harvest of new lives.*

I completely understand who Jesus is and am compelled to believe what He said. No thought or purpose of His can be held back or thwarted.

What I have learned through this process is that God has a mandate on my life. There is a ministry that is within me that needs to be birthed for a people group that the Lord has prepared. so that I can influence and speak life into them.

For that reason, I am Destined to Win! I have been chosen to be **Pierced for this Purpose!**

Notes On Overcoming:

Notes On Overcoming:

_____

_____

_____

_____

_____

_____

_____

_____

_____

Author Michele Saunders

Author Michele Saunders

Michele was born in Beth Israel Hospital, now Beth Israel Deaconess Medical Center, in Boston, Massachusetts, to the late Barry and Gail Monteiro. She is an only child, the only grandchild on her mother's side, and the oldest grandchild on her father's side. Talk about being a "Type A" personality!

Michele is a native and fifth-generation Bostonian, being able to locate and trace the history of her family in the book, "Twenty Black Families of Massachusetts," beginning with the story of her fourth great-grandfather, Aaron Josephs, who was a Whaling Ship captain from Bermuda.

Throughout her lifetime, Michele attended for periods of time and seasons, major houses of worship, which left lasting imprints upon her spiritual life, growth, and walk with Jesus. She is grateful for all the men and women of God who have taught, disciplined, poured into, sown tangible gifts into, prayed for, and shepherded her throughout her nearly fifty years of living. She gives God much thanks and praise for every person who has contributed to her positive growth both spiritually and naturally. Michele is the true embodiment of the adage, *"it takes a village."*

Michele is the owner of Michele's Editing Company. She started her early career years after graduating from Boston Latin School and earning her Bachelor of Arts degree in Journalism from the University of Massachusetts Amherst. As a newspaper copy editor, she has worked on News and Features desks at major newspapers around the nation, including the Minneapolis Star Tribune, the Boston Herald, and the Boston Globe. With the onset of financial troubles at the newspapers because of the rise of the Internet, Michele decided to shift into administrative work in higher education. Michele was a faithful worker in the posts she found herself in until illness decided to pursue and overtake her body. This is where her chapter begins.

During the pandemic, Michele earned her Masters of Arts in Christian Sales and Management from Newburgh Theological Seminary and is on track to be the second doctor on her mother's side and first on her dad's side. She is building additional income streams with the intent to benefit many and is accomplishing goals she set out to conquer before illness took hold of her body. In and through all things, Michele is grateful to God for His grace and mercy upon her life.

Connect with the author, Michele Saunders at:
Website: micheleediting.com
Email: MicheleSaunders2@gmail.com
Instagram: @micheleediting

Double for my Double-Trouble

What do you do when you have been prophesied to by multiple prophets, the same thing over time, wait on that word for one full decade, and then, when that thing comes to pass, it only stays with you for a brief moment?

What do you do when you get a life-changing illness that puts you face-to-face with your mortality in record time?

The same thing in both cases.
You worship the Lord.

In 1999, my husband and I semi-eloped, having been married before God by our former Bishop, before the church congregation after a beautiful Sunday service one Fall afternoon. About two months after our wedding, the first of about ten visiting prophets called us out before the congregation and told us that we would birth twins. They said repeatedly, in many different ways that our children would impact many for Christ and would-be philanthropists. At one point, this prophetic word was so consistent that congregants would scream and rejoice when this same word was repeated.

I would note in my journal each time that this word was given. I held on to it in my heart and stayed excited for the first year of my marriage because I knew that my children were sure to come. My faith waned a little though, as time continued past year one, and then onto year two, where I experienced my first miscarriage. But I held onto the prophetic word because I trusted God.

Fast forward to year five. I was age 32. I had recovered from my third miscarriage and gave my waiting over to God. My thing was that I knew that my babies would come. One thing I wasn't ready for was the "how."

During this time, it became painful for me to not have any "fruit," from my marriage. It seemed as if that one fact was magnified in my life. The Biblical story of Hannah (I Samuel 1) and her wait on God for her son Samuel became that much more relatable to me. Also, seemingly the devil used a few women with access to me, to be "Peninnahs" in my life also.

Some would mock the word that was slow to be fulfilled in my life. One woman, in the church, for example, even went as far as to wish me a "Happy Mother's Day," and then turn around and quickly rescind that greeting by saying to me, "Oh, that's right, you're not a mother. Sorry." I can tell you that things like that would cut me like a knife.

Even so, I kept the faith.

Fast forward to my ninth year of marriage. Out of the blue, my gynecologist asked me my thoughts about having children, and all related to the subject. She ran some initial tests and saw that I had two major fibroids blocking my womb. We finally got to the source of the miscarriages that had ended my pregnancies during their early stages.

The gynecologist recommended the removal of the fibroids, which required full surgery and reconstruction of my womb. I had this surgery on May 5, 2009. It took about two months to fully and properly recover from this process.

Sometimes the prophetic word spoken over our lives will come to pass, but not in the ways that we think. The time waiting is not wasted. Sometimes God might be clearing the way and setting the stage for that word's fulfillment to come to pass.

During my post-surgery appointment, my doctor recommended both me and my husband to the fertility clinic for further follow-up. This really was a surprise to me because I hadn't thought that I had needed that type of consult. Going through this process, it still hadn't occurred to me that the prophetic word about me having twins was happening. After rounds of tests, we were recommended and approved for In Vitro Fertilization. Our process to conceiving through IVF yielded twelve fertilized embryos.

On January 16, 2010, Baby Number 5 and Baby Number 8 (I had named them Grace and New Beginning) were implanted into my womb. Strange, but I knew the EXACT moment that they *stuck*. The realization hit me in the hospital bathroom that I was finally going to be a mom. To twins! The prophetic word was coming to pass. But my joy would soon be proven to be short-lived. I was 37. My pregnancy was dangerously high-risk with more than a few difficulties and complications from Day One.

Even so, I continued to go to work and do "normal" activities. The final straw though came with a severe hemorrhage in my fifth month that nearly took all three of us out. I landed on hospital bed rest in a high-risk maternity ward for the remainder of my pregnancy.

In the twenty-fourth week of my pregnancy, I went into full premature labor. My body had been slowly opening and getting ready for birth over time. So, by the time the first labor pain hit, I was ready to give full pushes. Iyesha was the first baby out. Doctors tried to keep Joseph in so he could live a little longer in the womb, but this was not feasible. He had to come out, too.

Both were born late in the evening on June 17, 2010. Joseph lived for two hours. He passed away on June 18, 2010. Iyesha lived for two days, passing away on June 19, 2010.

Numerous prophetic words and the ten-year wait ultimately yielded a two-day visit with my babies. But I wouldn't change this for anything. The process and recovery hurt a whole lot. But hindsight and prayerful reflection has shown me that God fulfilled all that He said he would do.

My twins came.

They also fulfilled the destinies and completed the assignments they were sent here to undertake. Joseph and Iyesha allowed me the honor of becoming their mom. They touched many lives for Christ. They are and will continue to be philanthropists in name.

At their funeral, two hundred and fifty people attended, and countless numbers either received salvation for the first time or rededicated their lives to Christ. A benevolence fund and nonprofit named The Joseph Issachar and Iyesha Jasmine Saunders Benevolence Fund and Nonprofit, where gifts will be given in their names to help various causes is being established.

My children also are being remembered among countless others who might read this book.

And my faith in God has been strengthened and solidified to greater levels.

One might think that I would have been angry at God. To the contrary! There was definitely a deep hurt because of the loss of my babies. Their passing left a void in me that will remain. But I feared God too much to be angry with Him.

I remember, however, a few days after the funeral, with my mourning and pain and sorrow being just as great as Day One of my children's passing, telling the Lord with tears streaming down my face that I loved Him more than anything – even my children. Strange, but I felt a breakthrough and healing. It is like I had had an "Aha!" moment.

I repented for pursuing the Lord for outward status symbols, including cute children. I rededicated my life to Him for real. This included being sure to give God my full "Yes," to the call of prophet. It was on this day that I understood the full cost of the call of God on my life and agreed to pay the cost for it. But I was happy for the opportunity to get it right.

I also understood what Jesus said in the scripture- *These things I have spoken unto you, that ye might have peace. In the world, ye shall have tribulation: but be of good cheer; I have overcome the world.* John 16: 33 (KJV)

Jesus even tells us that trouble - including the premature birth and passing of prophesied children - will come. But through Him with the right natural and spiritual supports, we can overcome all things, including immense sorrow and pain.

Fast forward six years to 2016. It is during this year and beyond, that I experience another cornerstone trial of my faith.

One minute, I am breathing fine. Then, next thing I know, I have a slight cough that graduates in a span of about one month to a hacking choke that leaves me gasping for air. I initially equated me being out of breath after movement, to being out of shape, and with me needing to lose a few pounds.

However, there was one event at home when I was so weak in my wrists that I kept involuntarily dropping items; I did not have enough strength to hold my grip. This prompted me to call an ambulance to get to the hospital for help. It was during this Emergency Room visit that a nurse (so grateful for the front-line nurses!) discovered that my gasping for air was because the oxygen saturation in my body had declined to dangerously low levels. Bottom line? I should have been on oxygen days before I arrived at the Emergency Room.

My hospital kept me on oxygen and as an inpatient for six weeks while they determined the best course of action and treatment for me. I was 44 at the time. I had been diagnosed with Rheumatoid Arthritis at age two and had battled many skirmishes with the disease. It was discovered, during my stay, that it was the Rheumatoid

Arthritis that had inflamed my lungs. It was also during my hospital stay that the doctors recommended that I have as quickly as possible a double lung transplant to remain alive.

This was August 2016. After the diagnosis and recommendation for transplant, I was initially released to a rehabilitation center to regain strength and then allowed to go back home. I embarked upon the process of enrolling as a transplant candidate and subsequently being cleared for transplant. All the while, my lungs continued to decline in strength and oxygen output.

The decline had gotten so severe over time, I decided to call an ambulance for help at midnight on November 6, 2016. I was told, once I got settled into my hospital room, that I would not leave the hospital until I "had new lungs." That period ended up being close to six weeks, culminating in me receiving my new lungs during a near twenty-four-hour surgery process on Saturday, December 17, 2016.

In November 2016, I was given a maximum of six months to live because of the rate of decline of my lungs. That was five years ago.

Here is what I did once I learned of the recommendation for transplant: I worshipped the Lord. I knew that the Lord would visit me and give me peace. It was in my worship that I came to a few things: not everyone is fit or recommended for transplant; and my process to transplant, which could have taken years, was moving at lightning speed in terms of days.

I knew that if the Lord brought me to this situation, that He would bring me through it. It was at this point that I had reminded Him of my "Yes," and stood in faith.

The diagnosis was scary. But a solution was offered. And I was willing to take it in faith.

None of this was in my plan. But somehow, I knew that the Lord was going to use this as a modern-day example of Him healing and making a way where there looked to be no way. So, I decided to trust God, because clearly to me in this situation, the only way out was-going *through!*

I can tell you that God wastes NOTHING.

When my babies passed, I initially thought, "What was the point of that?!?!"

But over time, God answered. It was to show:

The power of the true prophetic word.

The power of faith.

The power of loving God over everything.

This testimony of me waiting for my children to come, is also to encourage women currently on a difficult journey to motherhood.

My testimony is also to confirm the power of God in fulfilling His word.

Another major key that I learned through the process of my children coming to "visit," is that people fulfilling their destinies is not contingent upon our timelines, agendas, or schedules. My children came and accomplished all that they were assigned to do. It is just that their work was completed in an accelerated time frame. Conversely, my lungs also came at an accelerated pace. In and through all these things, God did all that He said He would do. He kept His word.

Isaiah 61:7-8, & 11: *For your shame, ye shall have double; and for confusion, they shall rejoice in their portion: therefore, in their land they shall possess the double: everlasting joy shall be unto them. For I the LORD love judgment, I hate robbery for burnt offering; and I will direct their work in truth, and I will make an everlasting covenant with them. And their seed shall be known among the Gentiles, and their offspring among the people: all that see them shall acknowledge them, that they are the seed which the LORD hath blessed. For as the earth bringeth forth her bud, and as the garden causeth the things that are sown in it to spring forth; so the Lord GOD will cause righteousness and praise to spring forth before all the nations.* Isaiah 61: 7-8, 11(KJV).

God has NOT forgotten about you. He is so mindful of you, although it may not look or feel like it. All throughout the wait for my children and my new lungs, the Lord God was working behind the scenes on my behalf to turn all the tough situations for my good.

It has been five years since that initial six-month ultimatum. This is ONLY God.

Although I kept in faith, I also had the right supports in place, including prayer partners, family members, and even a licensed counselor working on my behalf to make sure that I didn't fight any of my fights alone, for we really cannot, nor should we *do life* alone. We all need each other.

It is my strong prayer that not one person reading this, experience anything remotely like what has been briefly detailed in this chapter. It is also my prayer that as you navigate the really hard things in life, that you remember that God loves you, He is moving on your behalf, and that you must stand in faith, for all things are possible for them who believe. You will get through your hard things. I'm a living witness, eleven and then again five years later.

Thank you, Lord!

Notes On Overcoming:

Author Mischlane Melton

Author Mischlane Melton

Mischlane Melton was born and raised in Atlantic City, New Jersey. She has been residing in Las Vegas, Nevada for the last five years. Mischlane is the mother of two amazing young ladies, Jatirah 29, Janiyah 23. She's the Glammom to Little Miss Charli who's three years old, and the soon-to-be Glammom to baby boy, Judah, all currently residing in Las Vegas.

Mischlane grew up in a large family on both her mother and father's side and has always been family-oriented. So, moving to Las Vegas was a huge decision for her to make. While still living in New Jersey, Mischlane worked in the school district for about eight years as a paraprofessional and cheerleading coach, before deciding to explore the entrepreneurial world.

After starting several different business adventures, Mischlane was finally able to find her niche in the coaching arena. Mischlane was always a magnet for helping women and young ladies through many difficult experiences in their lives. While noticing some years later that this was something that kept her adrenaline pumping, that's when Mischlane discovered her life's purpose.

Mischlane is now the owner of Tribe of MelaniNation which represents the Voice of Uncomfortable for the Melanin Woman. She connects with women daily, helping them uncover and rediscover their

R. A. W. (Real Authentic Woman) selves through the Tribe Apparel, Coaching, and Healing Boutique.

Connect with author Mischlane Melton at:
instagram.com/tribeofmelanination
facebook.com/mischlane
info@tribeofmelanination.com

A Five-Year Bid

When we hear of someone doing a bid, most times we automatically imagine that person doing a jail or prison sentence, right? Most times, that is the case. Although I did experience a very, very short time behind bars, like a few hours, this isn't exactly the bid I'm speaking of. In fact, sometimes the weight of your life can be so heavy that it becomes unbearable. In that moment, you might feel that a prison bid would be easier to do than to continue to live your life.

When I was a little girl, five years old to be exact, my mother was having my baby brother. It was what I considered to be the most illuminating experience of my life. Why? Because, up until the age of five, I was the only child. My parents were both young when I was born. Being the first and only child, you get to have your parents all to yourself, along with many other things. When my brother was born all of that stopped. I was excited to have my brother; however, it changed my life in both a good way and a not-so-good way.

The good way of course, now I'd have a playmate, someone to grow up with and to boss around. However, the not-so-good way, changed my life forever. Nothing prepared me in any way, for what my life was about to be like. I had no idea the SHIFT that was taking place.

As I mentioned, my parents were young, like fourteen and sixteen years old. So of course, they still had some growing up to do, along with some other things, like partying. My mom was quite the girl growing up. She had lots of friends that also came with lots of enemies. She wasn't the real wild and crazy type; neither was she the fighting type. However, she was very attractive and attracted a lot of guys. I remember doing some things with my mom as a little girl. Unfortunately, though, that memory bank isn't too full.

Throughout most of my childhood years, I was able to be a little girl and do little girl things. However, while I was still young, I was responsible for doing some things that my mom would normally do, like taking care of my brother and making sure things around the house were in order. My mom liked to party, and most of the time, her partying included smoking and drinking. In the beginning, it was more of a casual thing. Later, as I moved into my preteen years, my mom's partying, smoking and drinking became a lot more serious. As a result, I had taken more of my mother's responsibilities. My brother was always the quiet, keep-to-himself kind of kid, so he was never a problem unless I made him one by being the annoying big sister. My brother also often spent time with his dad and uncles. At times, that was a big help.

Things started to get a little more demanding as I slid into my teenage years. My mom's drinking got heavier, and her attention was pulled away from me and my brother more and more. I didn't experience the mother-daughter relationship that I would have loved to have experienced. That is the reason that I'm glad I had the girlfriends that I had and still have. Although I didn't like to talk much about my home life and relationship with my mom, my girlfriends and I all had a thing or two in common we could share when it came to our relationships with our moms. A lot of times, it was these conversations with my friends that kept me going.

I was always a different kind of kid growing up, and I knew that. I also knew that I was afraid to be my "different" self because I didn't want to stand out or look different. I played with Barbie dolls until I was fourteen and then BOOM! After that, everything began to change. I could no longer be my different self, although sometimes I wish I had been, and so I started making myself fit in.

At fifteen, I started having sex, and at sixteen I was pregnant with my first child. Then I got to experience being a young mom, and then I didn't. I carried my son to term, gave birth, and then two weeks later he had died. The pregnancy itself was a traumatic experience, but the aftermath of my son's death was even deeper. Not knowing how to deal with something like that, I very easily picked up my feelings and emotions, packed them away, and moved on with my life. Or so I thought. About a year later, I was pregnant with my second child. Three short years later, my mom had now passed.

Prior to either of the three events, my mom and I had projected so much negative energy toward each other. At times her intoxicated self would make herself present when I would have friends over, and sometimes it would turn out really bad. Again, thankfully I had the friends I did; however, it was still embarrassing. Somewhere in between playing with Barbies to having sex and losing my first-born, I had not only contemplated suicide, but I had also attempted suicide! When my mom's drinking had gotten heavy, and her attention was pulled away more and more from me, I felt even less important. Yes, I say *even less important* because, going back to that little girl who wasn't the only child anymore, was the point where the feelings of insignificance began.

It started small. It wasn't really that big of a deal. During my early teenage years is when it started to deepen. Not having the attention at home, I went looking for it in other places like partying, boyfriends, and sex. I felt invisible, used, and taken advantage of almost all the time. That started me thinking that maybe it would be better if I wasn't here anymore. Luckily, my suicide attempt didn't work. I took a handful of pills, but nothing happened. After taking the pills, I discovered the pills were of a mild dosage and insufficient to do any harm. I knew deep inside that I didn't want to die. I also knew that, at that moment, I needed to feel noticed. I needed that attention and was willing, by any means necessary, to get it.

One season of good memories I do remember, was the year before my mom passed away. Things for my mom and I had started to lighten up. She had started having fewer intoxicating days, but at times, she lacked energy. We started to talk more. I remember days when I would go into her room and just lay across the bottom of her bed and rest my head on her ankles. We would lay and watch television and have a conversation. I wasn't too concerned about how much talking we did. Just being in her sober presence was good enough for me: it was a start.

I had moved out into my own apartment which was about seven miles from my mom. We didn't see each other every day anymore, but I would still go over to sit and spend time with her as often as possible. I guess it was good that I had moved out because, at times when my mother didn't want to be bothered or she decided to drink, it didn't affect me as much. This went on for about a year. One Sunday I cooked dinner and invited my mom over. I was getting prepared to go pick her up. When I called to let her know I was on my way, she said she was gonna stay home because she wasn't feeling too well. I was a little disappointed. However, I was okay with that and just took her a plate instead. I called and checked on her later that night before going to bed and then again, the next day. She said she was fine. A couple of days later, I received a call early in the morning from my aunt telling me that my mom was gone. Immediately, I broke. My whole world had just shattered.

All I could think was, "things were going so well and now she's gone." Once again, I was back in the same place. What do I do now? How do I pick it up from here?

I was twenty-one and for the next eighteen years, I went through life carrying all these packed bags. My bags were packed with loss, hurt, brokenness, and bitterness, to just name a few. I was numb. I buried my sorrows in sex and toxic relationships. I smiled heavy and hard to keep all the pain from seeping out. I kept busy and made myself available all the time to keep from feeling and dealing with the pain. Remember, I said we would choose to serve that physical bid because it just seems so much easier? Well, that's what I thought until I did my "Five Year Bid." Oh, wait, you thought all of that was my bid??

In 2009, I went to a doctor's appointment that turned my already shattered world upside down. I received a diagnosis that I'd expected to be the total opposite. I don't believe it actually had anything to do with the diagnosis itself. However, because I was already in a mentally depressed state that I wondered how much longer my smile would hide, just about any and everything that came my way could send me over the edge. During this time, I was in a relationship and when I left that appointment, he was the first person I called. After sharing the daunting news that I had just received from the doctor, his response was a traumatically low blow. "Why are you telling me?", was his response. That sent me right back to that little girl, and that young teen who felt invisible, only this time, the pain was much deeper.

For the next five years, 2014-2019, I had experienced all those same feelings of hurt, pain, loss, brokenness, bitterness, numbness and suicide, that I had packed in those bags, ten times more. My life for those five years was like, "The Walking Dead." My life got busier. The noise became louder. I became more available. All to keep from feeling. Then, the numbness grew deeper, and the suicidal voices came back. Louder and louder. I wanted it to stop. For good. I wanted it to be silent. My life was on autopilot, and I was merely existing.

I now had two daughters at this time, who had no clue that their mother was contemplating suicide. I couldn't wait for them to leave for school some mornings so that they didn't see me break. I remember one morning anticipating their departure. The moment my daughters left the house I had a complete mental breakdown. I was in my bathroom crying and asking God to please do something. I knew that at that moment I had nothing left. I had spent many of my days driving, wondering if I drove at full speed into a wall, would the impact kill me immediately or would I have to suffer through the pain? It was only because I knew my girls expected me to be there every morning when they woke up and every day when they returned home, that I didn't test my curiosity. I thank God for my girls.

Finally, the "Big Shift!" As I was just stepping into my forties, a lightbulb came on. I was literally at the end of my rope. When this light came on, my mindset began to change. I began to wonder what it would be like to take a chance on me. I knew that I had given myself away to everyone and everything, but I had never considered giving myself all of me. The thought became more and more intense the more I thought about it. So, I did. I decided to take that chance! I had no clue where to start, nor did I know what it would take. I figured if I can put so much time and energy into all the things, people, and places that I did over the years, I for sure could invest that time and energy into me. For the next eight years, that is exactly what I did. Today, I am still investing.

With everything that I had experienced and gone through, I realized and INNERstood that my only problem was a lack of SELF. Because I lost sight of who I was and in turn adopted and adapted all that surrounded me, I went through life lacking self-love, self-confidence, and self-worth. Without any of that, you so easily suck up and soak up all you can to feel seen and validated. What I know and have found is that suicide is real, depression is real, lack of self is real. What I also know and have found is that those things are ONLY as real as YOU make or allow them to be. We were created in the image and likeness of The Most-High, The Holy One, and that means we were created with all the tools we will ever need to be and become all that we so desire. There is nothing and there is no one that can stop us from BEING.

What I have learned and continue to learn daily is, everything that you need comes from within. The deeper you go within and clean up what's inside, the more peace you have, the more whole you become. We put a lot of time into the external things and the things we have no control over. We look for all the answers and reasons why externally when all the answers are right inside of us.

I know that you have been used and abused. I know you have been mistreated and taken advantage of. I know you are lost, broken, and bitter. I know you have given of yourself over and over again. I know you are always there for everyone else, and no one is ever there for you. I know. And, because I know, I want you to do me a favor. I want you to make the SHIFT. I want you to shift YOUR trajectory! Take your eyes off the things around you and shift them to the things inside of you. Take your hands off the things you cannot control and put them on the things that you can, YOU. Take your mind off the things that happened to you, the people that hurt you, and the places that no longer serve you and put it on the person, the place, and the thing that matters the most, YOU. I promise you, when you begin to shift and work your way from the inside out, your entire world begins to change. You've taken a chance on everything else around you. I'm challenging you to take a chance on YOU. No one owes you anything however, you owe yourself everything. Make up your mind and MAKE THE SHIFT!

Notes On Overcoming:

_____

_____

_____

_____

_____

_____

_____

_____

Notes On Overcoming:

_____

_____

_____

_____

_____

_____

_____

_____

Author Monique Evette Thomas

Author Monique Evette Thomas

Monique Evette Thomas was born in Florence, South Carolina, and was raised in Boston, Massachusetts. She graduated from Boston Latin Academy, and she earned her Bachelor of Science in Food and Nutrition, with a minor in English from Framingham State University. She loves The Lord, loves to read, likes to travel, enjoys listening to gospel music, is fascinated by science, technology, engineering, and mathematics (STEM), and loves to eat different cuisines, especially seafood, Caribbean, and Asian cuisine. Her career goals are to become a virtual assistant, nutritionist, food professional, and freelance writer of not only food and nutrition but also about being an overcomer in Christ and a sexual abuse survivor. She is single and currently lives in Brookline.

Connect with the author **Monique Evette** *at:* Monique.thomas880@gmail.com. *Instagram:* www.instagram.com/moniqueevettethewriter/.

I Just Wanted a Father

T hroughout my childhood, I longed for a "regular" family based on what I saw on various media, in my neighborhood, and at church - a mother, a father, and maybe a sibling or two. I had a mother, a grandmother, an uncle, an aunt, cousins, and a church family – but not a father. I felt like having a father was the big missing piece to my family puzzle.

I was born in the late 1970s in Florence, South Carolina to a teenage mother. From my understanding, she and my teenage father were not together when I was born. My mother and I, along with my grandmother and my uncle, moved to Boston, Massachusetts when I was a few months old. We lived on Holworthy Street in the Dorchester section of Boston, where a lot of our relatives lived.

When I was around two or three years old, my mother and grandmother joined an Apostolic church in the Roxbury section of Boston, not far from Holworthy Street. The pastor was an older lady who was a mother figure to us. A lot of the members were from Holworthy Street and hailed from various southern states, which I'm sure made my family feel at home.

I was five years old when I finally met my father during a visit to South Carolina. I recognized him from my mother's pictures and said, "Wow, he's handsome! I look just like him."

I was so happy I finally got to meet my father, and he seemed glad to meet me. We spent a lot of good times together. I met his mother – my other grandmother – along with many of his siblings and nieces and nephews. I was finally able to say that I HAD a father, like my cousins and the other kids at school.

When I was about eight years old, my mother and I went back to South Carolina. I got to see family members, and most importantly, I got to see my daddy again! We did even more activities, such as going to the movies (which was discouraged by our church), playing video games at the arcade, and eating great food – particularly that which he cooked at the Chinese restaurant where he worked. Then, more good news came; my parents got married a few months later when I was nine!

A few months after that, we moved out of my grandmother's place into my parents' own apartment. Over the course of years, my brother and two sisters were born. The fun continued when my father would play games like Jeopardy with me. Personally, great things were happening for me, as well. In the seventh grade, I enrolled in Boston Latin Academy, one of Boston's most prestigious exam schools. I also got more involved in the church by being the Sunday School secretary and teacher, usher, and choir member.

But then my father started acting strangely. When I began puberty, he'd come into my room, close the door behind him slightly, look at me long and hard without saying a word, and either would interrupt me from doing homework to do Kegel-like exercises on the floor or lay right next to me while in bed. I was just trying to be an obedient daughter, going by the scripture- *Honor your father and your mother, that your days may be long upon the land which the Lord your God is giving you.* "Exodus 20:12, (NKJV). So, I didn't question it. But I wondered why he did that. I began having a hard time going to sleep and would get up for school so tired.

As I got older, things got worse. My father became extremely obsessive about my appearance and my hygiene and would lose his temper whenever I or my mother made mistakes or didn't meet his expectations. He didn't allow me to wear makeup or jewelry per the teachings of our church. He didn't allow me to go anywhere but to school, church, the store with a family member, and to work without a bus pass. Mostly, he slept in the living room on the couch, wearing tattered shorts and an undershirt, with porn playing on the TV. When I was fifteen, he started touching me inappropriately. I froze up. I only knew about sex through movies and through the porn he was playing in the living room. I only knew to keep my legs closed so men wouldn't look at my privates and to be ladylike and polite.

When I turned sixteen, things got even worse. He ultimately stole my virginity…and my soul, heart, and mind were torn into pieces. He took me for his twisted pleasure to cure his "urges". I felt disgusted and used. My grades fell – I went from being an honor roll student to almost failing courses.

I started to fight back! So, when I was seventeen and in the eleventh grade, I decided to tell my mother, on that Friday during Memorial Day weekend. When I told her, she cried. She decided to confront him that night when he got home from work. He responded by yelling and accusing me of lying. My mother, my siblings, and I went to church that night. After church was over, my mother talked with our pastor about my accusation, and our pastor allowed my mother to use the phone to call the police to report my father and to have him removed from our home.

My pastor looked at me and said to me, "*Be strong*". Those words stuck with me... The ambulance came to the church to pick us up and take us to the hospital, where they confirmed that I was sexually abused. We stayed at a shelter where I was questioned about my ordeal.

That Tuesday, I returned to school and felt like a different person. I felt safer because he could no longer come into my room to abuse and disturb me, literally. However, I felt the after-effects of his actions. I fell into depression, sleeping for ten plus hours on end. I struggled with low self-esteem. I found myself easily startled by loud, sudden noises like balloons popping. I had dreams of him molesting me, and I felt sensations of my body parts being inappropriately touched.

Although I was free to travel and buy public transportation passes, that didn't stop my father from trying to rule the house even if he wasn't present. He still questioned why I went to events like a high school football game by myself. When I saw him on the bus, I refused to speak to him. My father would respond by saying, "You hurt my feelings and you are being disrespectful."

When I was turning eighteen and graduating from high school en route to college, I was expected to "grow up" and stop being a "crybaby", but I was woefully unprepared for adulthood. I was told to get help (which I did), but a part of me was in denial. I thought that if I just stayed busy, I would get better. Plus, I was still living with my immediate family because I didn't want to "backslide" and get pregnant. I really was just scared – of the opposite sex. I even chose to go to an all-women's college (which did offer me a decent financial aid package), but that didn't help with the internal scars I had. I dropped out after two years.

I entered my twenties, slowly on the road to recovery. I prayed to get closer to God, and I think those prayers helped me years later. I continued to do church work. I enrolled in a for-profit school and earned an associate degree in secretarial arts. However, I felt stunned when I saw my peers dating and starting families. I still felt like that awkward, misunderstood little girl who hadn't grown up. I allowed others, male and female, young and old, to control me and take advantage of me. I began looking at pornography on my own, to try to simulate that intimacy I craved and wanted on my own terms. Yet, I was trying to abstain from sex until marriage. I dressed in clothes that hid my figure, for the sake of being "modest". I didn't know how to be confident in myself. I tried to speak to guys with little success. Much to my chagrin, I got cat-called by older men on the streets.

When I was about twenty-six, I met my father's oldest sister. She had left home when my father was a baby; so, they didn't know each other very well. I visited her in Maryland, and she encouraged me to fix myself up, wear makeup and jewelry (yes, God was fine with it), and forgive my father so that I could heal. I honestly thought that I had forgiven him, but

I learned I had a long way to go. He was coming around again, trying to reconcile. My siblings were teenagers at that point, and our father was giving us money and having us come over to his place in Lynn, which is about ten miles south of Boston. I told him how the abuse was wrong and how I forgave him, and I asked him for permission to use his last name - "Thomas". I felt that I would have my daddy back!

A couple of years later, as I neared thirty, I decided to go back to school full-time to finish my bachelor's degree. I left my full-time job to live on campus at Framingham State, which was about twenty miles west of where I lived. However, tragedy struck when my grandmother passed away unexpectedly on September 11, 2008. She was the rock of our family. I felt like the wind had been knocked out of me. My father started coming to my mother's house, and eventually moved in, once again trying to control things. In her will, my grandmother left me in charge of her funeral, but I allowed my father to have his say-so regarding the details of her funeral and distribution of her possessions. I also allowed him to dictate when I should come home from school; he insisted that I needed to spend time with my family. I allowed him to have access to my bank account and my post office box. A friend told me that I was allowing him to control me. Her comment opened my eyes.

Soon mess hit the fan at home! One of my siblings refused to allow our father to be around her. To protect herself, she blocked her bedroom door. He accused her of being difficult and disobedient. That same sibling reported our father to her school, and once again, our father was kicked out of the house. I tried to talk to my pastor about the current situation, but she said that what happened to me was years ago, and it was time to let it go. My pastor also said that my sibling had nothing to do with what happened between me and my father. Among other things, this caused me to question whether I should continue being a member of my church. I also reflected on how I should have protected my sibling.

I told my aunt in Maryland about the events, and she told me I needed to file charges against my father. At first, I thought that reporting him was the wrong thing to do. My pastor had convinced my mother not to file charges. Our pastor said to my mother, "If you file charges, you will lose your children to the system! And to me, she said, "Monique, you need to let God handle it."

But I realized that I needed to file charges! In 2011, during my third year at Framingham State, I tried to do that, but the statute of limitations had expired. I was angry and had moments when I wanted to attack my father! I decided to cut ties with him; as a result, he accused me of not helping him.

I remember one encounter that turned my life around. When I visited a church with a friend, during my last year in college, a lady whom I didn't know, gave me a hug. Then she said, "Jesus wanted me to tell you that He loves you!" I had heard – "Jesus loved me", my whole life, but I began to doubt His love because of all I went through. I thought that I had to do things to earn His love, but I didn't. He loved me already! He loved me enough to die on the cross for my sins. Yes, even though I was sinned against, I also had sinned and had done things to others and to myself that weren't pleasing to God. But God forgave me and loved me. About a year after graduation, I fully dedicated my life to Christ, to have a relationship with Him not based on works, but on His work on THE CROSS!

When I did that, God opened my eyes to a lot and told me to let *victimhood* go! I needed more counseling – which I've been blessed to receive from good therapists. I'm learning about who Monique is and what she likes and doesn't like. I have better desires and goals: a better functioning nervous system, to be married and start a family, to have a better career, to help other people who have been abused, and more! I'm learning to not let fear overtake me, but to fill my mind with God's Word and positive affirmations. God has delivered me from looking at porn! He led me to find a great, Bible-believing church in Englewood, NJ which I livestream and hope to live near one day.

I wondered why my former pastor, who is now deceased, told me to "be strong" and "leave it in God's hands" instead of reporting to the authorities. She didn't want me to be bitter and be stuck as the victim. I also think that unfortunately, in the black community, sexual abuse is swept under the proverbial rug. We, in the black community, don't want our men to get in trouble with the police and go to jail since many of our people have been treated unfairly by the police. However, if a black person, or any person, harms their child, they need to face the consequences of the law, in order to protect other children from harm.

I realize that hurting people hurt people. Someone most likely abused my father, who in turn abused me. I no longer hate him, nor do I any longer want to seek revenge. I feel bad for him, and I pray for him. However, I cannot have a close relationship with him at this time because it's toxic. I believe that loving from a distance is a sign of respect.

Despite how my earthly father failed me, God has provided for me and is truly my Heavenly Father. I can say that He loves me and cares for me, and I'm on the right path! *When my father and my mother forsake me, then the Lord will take care of me.* Psalm 27:10 (NKJV).

Notes On Overcoming:

_____

_____

_____

_____

_____

_____

_____

_____

_____

_____

Author Tammy Vaughan

Destined to Win Series Visionary

Author Tammy Vaughan

Destined to Win Series Visionary

Pastor Tammy Vaughan serves as senior pastor of Freedom Christian Center, located in Burlington, NC. She is a wife, mother, and grandmother of five. Pastor Tammy holds a master's degree in social work and is a Licensed Clinical Therapist and an Addictions Specialist. She is the CEO of Gracepoint Recovery Services, LLC, where she and her team will assist youth and adults with mental health or substance use issues.

Pastor Tammy is a certified Life Coach and the CEO of Bhealed Coaching. For the past ten years, she has coached and counseled hundreds of women and men to work through deep trauma and heal their wounds to have life-changing breakthroughs. In order for this to happen in a person's life, Pastor Tammy equipped herself to offer different strategies for healing. She believes this is the formula needed for a person to reach their next level in life.

Moreover, Pastor Tammy is a servant and leader who predicates her life on following Jesus Christ. She loves helping others reach their full potential and believes that everyone should be given the opportunity to have the best quality of life.

With a passion to help women and men to share their stories to impact the world, Pastor Tammy launched the **DESTINED TO WIN** book series, including volumes one-four: *Volume 1: An Antidote to Life, Volume 2: We Pushed Past It, Volume 3: Broken to Unbreakable,* and now *Volume 4: Pierced for a Purpose.* Her desire to celebrate the tenacity and resiliency of God's people has started a global movement of overcoming and empowerment.

Her Motto: To make a great life one must give to others.
~ Winston Churchill

To connect with Author & Visionary Pastor Tammy:
www.destinedtoinspire.com & www.Bhealedcoaching.com
Email: destinedwinner2020@gmail.com
Facebook Groups: www.facebook.com/groups/bhealedcoaching/ or
https://www.facebook.com/groups/winningwithwinners/
Instagram: www.instagram.com/bhealedcoaching

Pressed but Not Crushed

We are hard-pressed on every side, but not crushed; perplexed, but not in despair; persecuted, but not abandoned; struck down, but not destroyed." 2 Corinthians 4:8-9 (NIV)

This is a chapter that I was very eager to write; **Pressed but Not Crushed**. WHEW! Anything that is pressed would surely be crushed to the natural eye, but in the spirit, being pressed will not cause you to be crushed. What a MIGHTY God we serve!

The bible says: **"We are hard-pressed on every side, but not crushed; perplexed, but not in despair; persecuted, but not abandoned; struck down, but not destroyed."** (2 Corinthians 4:8-9) Those final words...**BUT NOT DESTROYED!!** Good God! I could just dance all around my room! I am NOT destroyed!! You know how exciting that is, to know that no matter what we go through, we will not be destroyed. I don't know if you read the first D2W book, where I talked about a very painful betrayal that I experienced from people that I loved and trusted. In that chapter, I share how I thought I was going to lose my mind, and that my heart would never heal. Then, I remembered this scripture. **"We are hard-pressed on every side, but not crushed; perplexed, but not in** *despair; persecuted, but not abandoned; struck down, but not destroyed.*" My prayer is that as you continue to read this chapter, it will prepare you for the pressing and the crushing so that when the storms of life begin to rage in **YOUR** life, you will have a solid foundation upon which to stand.

When reading the scripture, it is quite evident that Paul is so weak, tired, and ready to give up, yet God delivered him again and again. He used miraculous means and natural means to bring Paul through the worst times of his life. Throughout Paul's entire ministry, he suffered many trials and tribulations for the sake of being a follower of Christ. He was **stoned, beaten, imprisoned, shipwrecked, and betrayed**. There were times where he didn't have food, no sleep, and no place to live. Yet not one time did he ever speak of God forsaking him. Want to know why? Because God will **NEVER** forsake His children. Did you hear me? I said, "God will never leave you." As I studied the life of Paul, it seemed that he was fighting a losing battle. Have you ever felt like you were fighting a losing battle? Everything that could go wrong did, and there you are, standing and wondering where is God. I want you to know that He is right there with you. Scripture tells us, "*Be strong and of a good courage, fear not, nor be afraid of them: for the LORD thy God, he it is that do go with thee; he will not fail thee, nor forsake thee*" *(Deuteronomy 31:6).* This scripture has brought me through many of trials. I remember the times when I couldn't feel God, but I knew He was right there with me.

Beloved that are so many men and women, in the bible, who struggled with being hard-pressed, with being perplexed, with being persecuted, and even struck down. Yes, the godly men and women that you read about experienced depressed feelings, emotional grief, and times of despair.

Here are a few examples to show you that YOU'RE NOT THE ONLY ONE...

- Joseph was hated by his brothers and thrown in a pit. *(Genesis 37:24)*
- Job lost everything and cursed the day he was born. *(Job 3:1-26)*
- Daniel was thrown into a lion's den. *(Daniel 6:16)*
- Hannah was ridiculed because she couldn't conceive a child. *(1 Samuel 1:6)*
- Shadrach, Meshack, and Abendego were thrown into a fiery furnace for not bowing to another God. *(Daniel 3:19 &20)*

Finally, let's look at our Lord and Savior, Jesus the Christ. Look what he went through just for you and I. Mark (14:65) shares, *"Some began to spit at Him and to blindfold Him, and to beat Him with their fists, and to say to Him, "Prophecy!" And the officers received Him with slaps in the face."* WHEW!! MY GOD!! That scripture really does something to me! When I think of what Jesus had to go through for me, I get very emotional. When I think of how He took it all for me, I am so grateful to be a child of the King.

Hard Pressed

Let's talk about being **Hard-Pressed** for a moment. What does it really mean to be hard pressed? I know that you think because sister-so-and-so didn't speak to you this morning at church, you're being _hard pressed_. I know you think because a few folks are gossiping about you, you're being _hard pressed_. OOOPS, I hate to burst your bubble, but being _hard pressed_ has nothing to do with those examples. Being **"Hard-Pressed"** literally means we are pressured to give up, to be discouraged, to quit, to throw in the towel, and give up on everything, even God. Think about a bottle of olive oil that we cook with. In order for us to receive the oil, the olives had to be pressed and crushed.

We all have these pressures, sometimes in our lives. There might be the pressure of being married when you can't see eye-to-eye on some issues, the pressure of your supervisor blowing up at you because they are having a bad day or your boss giving a deserved promotion to someone else. What about the pressures of your past crowding your mind to the point that you can't seem to forgive yourself? Not only are we hard-pressed, but this 2 Corinthians verse says, _"On every side"_ which means- all around us. I know in my life, I felt like the pressure was all around me. How could I escape it? When I look to the left and to the right and there it was crushing me. There were times where my chest wouldn't expand for me to breathe because the pressure was so heavy.

The pressure weighing you down can come from all directions- pressure from your family, friends, the job, the ministry, and your business. Do you know that feeling? Have you experienced that type of pressure? I know I have!! I find that it's not just my ministry, my finances, or my job but it was also those close friends, who I trusted, that turned their backs on me. What about your family? Here you are trying to save the world and your children are acting like they just bought an express ticket to hell. All you can say is, **"WHEN WILL THIS STOP! I HAVE HAD ENOUGH!"**

While we are hard-pressed on every side, this scripture also has a promise in the next few words... **but not crushed!!** Beloved, please understand that the pressing is a process that no one wants to experience. Especially if you are in ministry. Allow me to be extremely honest with you, there were times, in my life, that the pressure was so bad that I contemplated checking myself into a psychiatric hospital! I just knew there was no way I was going to come out of my situation. Over and over, God proved me wrong.

The Crushing

Isaiah 53:5 states, **"But He was pierced for our transgressions, He was crushed for our iniquities; the punishment that brought us peace was upon Him, and by His stripes, we are healed."** Read that again. **By His Stripes, we are HEALED.**

Listen, let me tell you firsthand, no one and I do mean NO ONE wants to experience the crushing of their heart by someone they trusted. No one wants to be married for 20 years and your husband walks in and tells you, *"I've found someone else."* No one wants to hear, *"you have 6 months to live."* However, what we must understand is that being crushed, in deep places, happens to the best of us. It doesn't matter if you've been with the Lord for five days or five years. It just seems to be part of the rhythm of this thing, we call life. I know it's not fair. I know that you didn't deserve what they did. I know that it pains you to think about how they could betray you in such a manner.

I know you may be saying, *"What did I do wrong?"* or *"Why has God allowed me to go through such hard times?"* For a few years, I said to myself, *"Does He not care about me?"* Come on, tell the truth, and shame the devil, you know you asked those same questions. To be honest, you know you have felt a little something like this. I've also wondered if others were experiencing these hard times as frequently as I was. I mean, come on. No one is taking pictures of those **crushing** moments and posting them on Facebook or Instagram.

Here is what I have learned in my 20+ years on this Christian journey. Be careful about asking all these questions and questioning God. Just remember that the enemy can hear you too. He will say things like; *"God doesn't love you just look at what you are going through."* *"Why would a God who loves you allow your baby to die."* *"Look at your unsaved friends, who aren't going through adversity like this."* But you say, you are a servant of Jesus, and yet you are going through the worst times of your life. Don't allow the enemy to have these conversations with you. Silence the chatter and focus on His promises!!

I believe with all my heart that the breaking, the crushing, and the pressure happen because it was allowed by God. Now I know if you are anything like me, you are saying, *"but why would God allow this to happen?" "Why would he allow them to hurt me in such a manner?"* You see, God allows the breaking because He and He alone has the power to put us back together. When God is in it, we come out stronger, wiser, better, NOT bitter, miserable, and angry. As Marvin Sapp says, *"We never would have made it without God."* There's nothing that God won't do for His children. Trust me, our Heavenly Father knows what's best for us. I know in the old church they would say things like, *"Baby don't question God. We shouldn't question his plans for us, he made us, he gave us life. His will (not ours) will be done."* But come on. We need to know if we have what it takes to survive the hurt, the betrayal, the divorce, or the death of our only child. We need to know. Enquiring minds want to know!! So, I asked Him.

On August 14, 2021, I contract Covid 19 and two days later, my entire family was diagnosed with Covid. I remember when I was at my lowest and all six of us were struggling with the sickness. All I wanted to know was… *am I going to MAKE IT OUT alive.* I asked Him and He sent me to this scripture: **Jeremiah 30:17 "But I will restore you to health and heal your wounds,' declares the LORD."**

Beloved, listen, life is going to crush you. There is nothing you can do about that. The crushing will cause you to ask God, *why me??* I want you to truly understand the value of the crushing. The crushing is a process of life that must take place. Let's admit this: as believers, we are looking for God to release the rewards; the big house, the fancy car, the fine husband, and those perfect children. We never want to experience the crushing that could make us question the very God that we serve.

I want you to know that through every pain, God is building a warrior. You are the one that God knows He can count on. He knows that you won't throw in the towel when things get tough. The crushing makes you tough. The crushing builds character, it builds a warrior who can withstand the attacks of the enemy. I suspect that you know the tear-filled place from which I speak. I suspect the crushing has brought you to your knees. Nevertheless, **YOU MADE IT OUT!!!**

Also remember this, the ones that God has a HUGE assignment for are the ones that experience the **MOST** crushing.

Pierced for a Purpose

The main reason for the title of this book was because of the **piercing.** The piercing made me who I am today. I experienced God on a whole other level through my many trials.

You can't let your fear, betrayal, pain, etc. hold you back from your destiny. There is **PURPOSE** in you. You see, the enemy is focused on your purpose. He will torment and taunt you to get **you** to forget that **you** are a person of POWER and **PURPOSE.** There is greatness inside of you because the greater one lives on the inside of you (1 John 4:4). The unfortunate thing about this is that some people don't know it. They don't know the magnitude of the power that they possess. They don't know that God has equipped them for **GREATNESS.** I will admit, life makes it very hard for us to believe that we have a **PURPOSE** because we are constantly bombarded with adversity.

If you survived anything in life, it's because you have a **Destiny**, you have **PURPOSE.** What's sad is that a lot of people don't know their life's purpose. They struggle with the questions, *"What is my purpose? Why did God create me?"* The bible tells us that God created us in His image and likeness *(Genesis 27:1).* Why did God create you? I'm so glad you asked!

Number 1 - God created you to fill you with His precious spirit. .

Number 2 - God wants you to be a blessing to others. In other words, the purpose of your life is to serve, show compassion, and help others.

There is one thing that I do know, while you are trying to figure out your life, God has the answer. He can organize your life if you allow Him to. He can fill the empty/lonely spaces in your heart with hope, strength, and power. He will/can order your steps and direct you on the right path. He can brighten your life and give you purpose. God created you to be like Him, full of love, full of passion, full of bravery, full of confidence, full of power, and full of His Holy Spirit. He created us in His image. Beloved, you have a purpose even if the piercing tries to make you think/feel you don't.

As I close this chapter, I want you to pray this prayer with me...

Father God in Heaven,

I have been crushed and the emotions of it all have been troubling my life. I pray that as you and I work through this pain and these trials together, you will restore me back to complete wholeness. Father, I know that you will heal my heart, mind, and soul so I can rejoice in you. Father fill me with the light of your Spirit so I can arise from this painful state. Teach me to cast every care upon you. Fill me with your joy, love, and peace. Thank you for allowing me to survive some of the most painful experiences so I can share with others of your healing power. In Jesus' name, I pray, Amen.

You are Destined to Win...

Notes On Overcoming:

Author T. Angie Pullum

Author T. Angie Pullum

T. Angie Pullum was born and raised in Boston, Massachusetts, and has been an administrator in higher education for over 25 years. She holds a Bachelor of Science in Information Technology which has been vital in her career in virtual teaching and learning. Some of her personal interests include writing, digital spoken-word, content creation, and mental wellness advocacy. These are all personal passions of hers which she plans to merge into a single niche that will impact, encourage, and empower women and mothers of any age.

Angie is blessed to be a mother of five and a grandmother of two. As a single parent, family is her strength and her anchor. Her goal has always been to work hard and be an example for her family of independence, resilience, and determination. In that effort, some of her own personal dreams—like becoming a published author—sat quietly on the sidelines hoping to never be completely forgotten. When the *Destined to Win: Pierced for a Purpose* opportunity showed up, she jumped at the chance to finally pursue a dream that had been deferred long enough.

She has always wanted to write and be of service to impact others, but first, she had to go through her own life's experiences. She says, "God's timing is always perfect. The highs and lows of my life come so that I am able to meet others where they are and relate to reach them."

Connect with author, **T. Angie Pullum:** on Instagram at: https://instagram.com/afterwordwithangie/ or by emailing afterwordwithangie@gmail.com

Reclaiming My Voice

When I first heard *pierced for a purpose*, I instantly thought of being punctured in terms of wounding. As an avid fan of superhero movies, I followed through on that thought in my mind's eye towards the superhero, at the height of the battle, being pierced...being wounded. Even with a movie, you can feel your emotions rising, hoping, "Get on your feet! You can do it! Fight!" Is the superhero done for? Or will the superhero dig down deep, letting out that infamous cry, and find that last ounce of strength to become victorious in what is, at that moment, a fight for their life and probably the lives of others. So, as I continued to let the focus- *pierced for a purpose,* move about through my mind and ultimately through my heart, I began to open to the process. In my own life, I am the superhero. I have fought many battles. Some I have won, some I have lost, some I am still fighting. Then, it became a matter of what battle to share. Which battle do I feel has been a fight for my life that can impact others if I only allow myself to share? In that battle, was I done for, or did I dig deep and cry out to find that last ounce of strength to become victorious?

I have found that opening up the past can be painful. In my journey of healing, I realize that our origin plays a major part in who we are and why we are where we are. That's not to say that nothing can be changed, that origins keep things the same, no. But we all start from somewhere and our pain also starts from somewhere. As I embarked on my journey of healing, I seemed to have hit a wall. I couldn't get past this wall. In consistent, therapy to manage depression and anxiety, I had talked about every recent challenge and tragedy I could think of. So, I didn't know how much more open I needed to be to feel myself press past that wall to reach another level of understanding about my life, my passion, and my purpose. Surely, everything I was going through had to be for a reason. But what was the reason and why did it feel like it was running from me each time I thought I was getting close to it? So, I considered the fact that I kept trying to work on what was immediately in my heart and immediately on my mind as challenges in life. I began to wonder, as honest as I think I am, had I been very honest with myself about what I had gone through and how it affected me. Suddenly, I found myself disappointed with a lot of people, including my mother. Almost to the point that I didn't want to talk to her—and I love and respect my mother more than anybody in this world. So, the next time I had my appointment in therapy, I decided to explore my disappointment... even anger, I can admit that. The first words that left my mouth were, "Things happened to me when I was younger. I didn't feel protected, and I never felt safe or encouraged to talk about those things, so I never felt supported. I feel that truth stole my voice and I have been silent about so many things, that I have lost count." I promise you when I shared that, I felt that wall crack. I can't even describe in words what I experienced, and I didn't want anyone to think I was completely "out there", lost on my own. I realize that God has a plan for me, and I was never on my own even though I felt that way.

My voice. Those two words make me SO EMOTIONAL. As a creative person who is very expressive, writing and speaking come most naturally to me, out of all the many ways that I display my creativity. So, can you imagine how it felt to live life voiceless and in silence? Sure, I wrote in my journal for years, which I now realize was my therapy before therapy. What it is now, is another person there supporting me while I work out whatever I need to. Of course, I would vent here and there with my friends, especially the ones who were single mothers like me, and could understand. Even then, I didn't feel comfortable saying everything I was feeling about other things that had nothing to do with parenthood. So, when do I feel like I lost my voice? I was about 11 years old. Although I would never forget what happened to me, it has been buried for years until recently. Once I committed to uncovering my source of pain, my mother suddenly displayed a picture of me in her house that I felt was me around that age. When I tell you my mind was blown away at how much of a coincidence that absolutely was NOT, I knew that it was time to heal the loss of my voice by connecting to and protecting that brave little girl in the picture. I was going to have to do it even if it felt embarrassing, or shameful to me; or even if it made others feel embarrassed or shameful or guilty. There was a box of trauma, in the darkest part in the back of my mental closet. I am still brave, so it is time to open that box.

When school would let out, I would go straight home. I was a latchkey kid, so I knew the routine. When I got off the school bus, I headed home, locked the door, stayed inside, and didn't let anyone in or answer the door. Those were the rules and I followed them without opposition or difficulty. Until this one day. I was a homebody and I felt comfort, relaxation, and safety at home. I was a very laid-back, reserved kind of little girl. If something didn't bother me much, I didn't think much about it. So, things often were easygoing; but I would speak up when I had to. That internal system was fine until my mother had a boyfriend that she eventually trusted enough to allow him to be at our home, even when she wasn't there. I am going to do my best not to interject my current adult self too much, as I relay this experience, but what happened to me, understandably makes me extremely angry.

One day, I came home from school like any other day, and although I don't recall the details vividly (either due to survival mode or because it's been a very long time or both), he was either there already or he came to the house after I got home. I remember him being particularly chatty towards me and unusually nice. I didn't know what was going on, but my very young intuition knew enough and burned it in my mind enough to observe that he was particularly "nice". The reason he was behaving that way was because he began molesting me, touching me very inappropriately on my chest and between my legs. I try very hard to recall what I was thinking the first time he put his hand on my shoulder and rubbed my back, which was the action that led to even more inappropriate touching, but I can't recall much. All I can say is that I was 10 or 11—I had never been exposed to sexual things or even told about the "birds and the bees" or things little girls need to know to protect themselves in this predatory world. I was confused and rightfully had NO FRAME OF REFERENCE at that age to process and understand what happened to me! It didn't feel right, and I wanted it to stop but I didn't know how I was supposed to make it stop. Avoiding him was not working. He was my mother's boyfriend, someone that seemingly made her happy, so I didn't know how I was supposed to bring something to her that I at least knew would be upsetting even though I didn't know the adult magnitude of what that upset would be. Until I could figure out what to do, I would just put it out of my mind, go to school, and try to avoid him.

Every day, from then on, which wasn't going to be long, I dreaded getting off that school bus to go home. "Please don't let him be there," I would think. "Please let my mother come home right after me." Every single day, those were my thoughts and feelings. EVERY SINGLE DAY. As an adult, I wonder if my anxiety started there or doubled in size here. I never considered going outside or hanging out after getting off the school bus. For years, the rules were my routine, and that was to go home. I did what I was supposed to do even when it felt like the devil was in the house waiting for me. One day, I got up the courage to tell my mother. I don't even recall the details of that very much, but *he* definitely was no longer around when I told my mother. What I do recall is some arguing and then the devil wasn't in our house anymore. Whether that all occurred on the same day, I also don't recall. I just knew that he was gone, and I didn't have to worry about him touching me anymore. I used my voice! I dug deep for that ounce of courage, and I was triumphant. So how come instead of gaining more voice, I lost *all* my voice. My anxiety grew by leaps and bounds every single day as I worried about that man being in our house. When I spoke up, I was courageous but the arguing between adults and the "break up" energy that followed added to my trauma. I felt I had made more bad things happen by speaking up.

I wasn't old enough to realize that I had advocated for myself, as I should have, and that I should never quit doing that. No one told me that I had done the right thing. I did not get the support a child should have gotten after a situation like mine. No one assured me that I had done nothing wrong, to have been treated like that by an adult. No one told me that I could begin to feel safe again, or that I was brave for speaking up about the abuse. Finally, no one asked, "How are you feeling? Are you OKAY?" Instead of standing in bravery and advocacy, I felt like speaking up had created new problems. It was there, in that confusion, that I began *learning* to do whatever keeps other people from getting upset, and that involved me shutting up throughout life in situations of conflict, even when I really did have A LOT to say. As I got older, I didn't know how to release myself from that *stifle* as I call it. I don't want to make things about race, but in the black community, we suffer greatly from minimizing, not addressing, and not healing trauma. Then add to that, the lack of access and equity in quality care, and the problem is severe. I understand, now as an adult, how rooted in history and slavery, our trauma responses are. However, that understanding does not change the fact that the little girl, who was me, needed what she didn't get it. As a result, I developed very poor coping mechanisms and adopted silence as my habitual response. My primary comfort became, and still is, food. Then, following a family tragedy, for a period longer than I care to admit, to cope, I turned to alcohol. I am thankful alcohol is no longer a part of my story.

Being molested was a **pierce** to my voice, my safety, my self-esteem, and my self-value. Throughout my life, I continued having difficulty trusting myself and my intuition. Now, after all these years, I can look back with hindsight and SEE exactly when my intuition was guiding me; but not trusting it, resulted in me not honoring myself. Finding my voice again has been the longest battle this superhero ever fought! During this battle, I took measures such as strengthening my faith in God and exercising for my overall health, that gave me a second wind. Yet, there were times when I would revert to thinking negatively and having poor health habits. It felt like I would NEVER get anywhere until I accepted that I have been **pierced** in many ways **for a purpose** and that God has not given me a testimony to be ashamed of. In fact, He has given me a testimony that can impact so many people; I am submitting to His will. During the pandemic, I went to God for a one-on-one bootcamp! I was desperate. The *stifle* is stale. It's tiring, y'all. I'm over it! Our boot camp training began with disarming the fears I told Him that I have, which all stem from the spirit of anxiety: perceptions adopted about failing and letting people down in my life. God knew and understood the embarrassment, shame, and self-doubt I felt when I became a teen parent. I told Him about the negativity that I received and that I did not feel supported. I was kicked out at a young age and left alone to deal with my tough situations. There were many tough situations. Boot camp was intense as God, and I talked through them.

God needed me to know what I am talking about before He could truly use me, and so my voice has returned. The more I fearlessly open up about myself and share with others, the more I heal. Now, God needs me to work on my delivery, and he also needs me to BE a demonstration of His works. That is where I AM... working on what I dub my personal ABCDs:

- **appreciation** for life and an **attitude** of gratitude
- recognizing that I am **blessed** and **becoming** who I am meant to be
- being **consistent** and **committed** to myself
- being **disciplined** and **determined** to succeed

I am His work in progress. I have wished I could hop into a time machine and change some event that left me *pierced* and in pain. However, I have learned that instead of falling victim to *stifle* and feelings of mental and emotional paralysis, I must turn my pain into my power. I must allow God to train me for the battles of this life. Whenever we come up against unimaginable difficulties in life, we must know and believe that we can turn to God for His strength and for us to renew our minds so that we can dig deep for that mustard seed of faith, face our fear, and do what, in the flesh, we think is the impossible.

In the day when I cried out, You answered me, and made me bold with strength in my soul. Psalm 138: 3 (NKJV)

Notes On Overcoming:

A BOOK COMPILATION

DESTINED to WIN

Volume 4

Pierced for a Purpose

Thank you for
your support.

shero publishing

Made in the USA
Middletown, DE
29 May 2022

66346648R00126